Living With My Father

A *Study of Prayer*

Living
With My Father

A Study of Prayer

Written and Illustrated

by

Sherlie Rowe

QUALITY PUBLICATIONS
P.O. BOX 1060
ABILENE, TEXAS 79604

ISBN: 0-89137-808-1

DEDICATED

*TO ALL THOSE WHO LOVE
MY FATHER AND BRING HIM
JOY BY SEEKING HIM.*

"The Lord bless you and keep you;
the Lord make His face shine upon you
and be gracious to you;
the Lord turn His face toward
you and give you peace."
(Numbers 6:24-26)

PREFACE

Dear Reader,

Living With My Father has grown from a series of five lessons given at a ladies retreat on Prayer. God blessed our weekend together with growth in our individual relationships with Him. We found our relationships here on earth strengthened, restored and more warmly bound together in a climate of prayer and acceptance.

The book is written so that it can be used in three ways: a personal private study, for ladies' classes and for retreats.

FOR PERSONAL STUDY

If you choose to make a personal study, you can find new depths in your relationship to the Father by spending time adventuring at your own pace through the pages titled, For The Seeker. The Prayer Workshop suggestions for meditations and exploration are planned to aid your growth in communication with your Father.

FOR LADIES' CLASSES

If you are a ladies' class teacher, you already know the difficulty of your task in teaching a group with a wide spectrum of spiritual needs. Hopefully, this study will meet each person where she is in her prayer life and lead her to grow closer to the goal of perfection. The pages, For The Seeker, could be used as homework and springboards for group discussion. It is in a climate of prayerful working, studying and sharing that true fellowship develops which is invaluable to unity in Jesus.

The Prayer Workshop times are built around the Word and our personal prayers as a dialogue between each lady and her Lord. Ladies seem to especially enjoy the planned silent times of meditation. We have so few quiet hours that "just happen". Wives and mothers struggle for alone times with God to study and pray.

For the group meditation times, let the ladies go wherever they choose in the building or grounds. A pre-assigned person calls the group together by beginning a familiar, appropriate hymn which the ladies join as they return. No words are spoken during this time (a true discipline for a female?) On the days you are to have Workshop, have leaders prepared to guide groups of five to eight ladies. It is best for this study to keep the groups the same for the five periods of Workshop hours. Your leaders' primary responsibilities are to draw out of each group member her inner strengths to share, to be the group servant by opening herself to listen to and guide her group and to believe in each person as a valuable, dignified child of God worthy of respect. As the leader is able to lose herself in serving the group, something begins to happen for her and the group. Because she seeks only God's will for those she serves, her own personality and opinions are laid aside and the Lord can work through His word and Spirit to change lives.

The Ladies' Class Teacher will find this a flexible study that she can mold to her methods or change to suit her class needs as she sees them.

FOR A LADIES' RETREAT

Should you desire to use the book as a ladies' retreat, the lessons were originally built around the combination of the chapters into five lessons, designated as Parts I - V in the study. The suggested time length for Workshop hours could be increased in a retreat setting.

A one-day spin-off retreat was planned by the women of one congregation built around Part IV only. Your own ideas will grow as you pray about your group and let God lead you to best fill their personal needs.

The limit of our growth in our prayer lives is restricted only by our knowledge of God Himself and our faith. We need to break down the barriers that inhibit our relationship with our Father, but first we must identify them. Some of us speak to God as we did to our parents in childhood by telling Him what we think He wants to hear and avoiding any painful disclosures. When our children write to us or speak to us, telling us only what they know we can approve, the communication leaves us feeling empty, unable to share in their lives. It is almost as if they recited, "Mary had a little lamb". We want to plead, "After all I've done for you, after all the years of loving, can't you trust my love to bear anything you have to say?"

Some of us pray with little understanding of God's love. We are like the two-year-old who doesn't cry in class if allowed to hold her mother's purse, because she knows her mother won't leave her purse, completely unaware of her own preciousness to her parent. We pray beautiful, scriptural prayers, holding our Bibles as our anchor and hope, but not allowing God the closeness of a sharing of our inner selves bared to His love and guidance with eager open arms.

Beloved, we have wanted to be serious about growing in the grace of prayer. Somehow this wonderful privilege is pushed aside in our busy lives, relegated to a less important, unplanned, hurried corner. We sincerely plan someday "when life isn't so hectic", to give prayer more thought and study. Satan is busier and smarter than we are! Satan turns our values upside down, ruthlessly squeezing the joy, the blessings that could be ours from our days, leaving the dry peel of frustration, loneliness and vague hunger for an unidentifiable something.

Our Abba Father offers us the treasure of wisdom we need to live victoriously in Jesus. He is our Creator and He alone can change our characters to be like His Son, preparing us for heaven. He loves us more than we can begin to understand. As His daughters, let's join hands and hearts to grow in vital communication with our Living Lord. Our study will reveal God in intimate ways to bring our relationship from the formality of near strangers to the freedom of Father - daughter dialogue. Bit by bit for the rest of our earthly lives we will be learning to open our arms ever wider to eagerly share our inmost selves. As we study and pray, we will become more nearly the wives and mothers we long to be. Best of all, we can be changed to be a strength and blessing to the church, God's family, and a light to the world, made sensitive by His guidance and work in our minds and hearts.

May God use us all to glorify Him.

Sherlie Rowe

JESUS' TEACHINGS ON PRAYER

Luke 11:2-4 — The example prayer

Luke 18:1-8 — The parable to encourage us to persevere in prayer and not give up hope.

Luke 18:9-14 — The attitude of acceptable and unacceptable prayer

Luke 19:45,46 — His attitude toward those who prevent prayer in others.

Mark 11:22-25 — Effective prayer is based on total trust in God.

Matthew 6:5-14 — The prayerful heart must be humble, sincere.

Matthew 7:7-11 — Earnestness in prayer

Matthew 7:21,23 — Saving prayer is the prayer offered by those who live according to God's will.

Mark 14:38 — Directive for strength under trial.

Luke 20:47 — Warning against pretense in prayer.

JESUS' PRAYER LIFE

Luke 3:21	Prayed after baptism.
Luke 6:12	Prayed alone on the mountain all night before the morning He chose the twelve.
Luke 9:18	Prayed immediately preceeding posing the important question to the twelve, "Who do ye say that I am?"
Luke 9:29	Prayed on the mountain, accompanied by Peter, James, and John, as He sought strength and assurance concerning the cross soon to be His (v. 31).
Luke 11:1-4	Praying when the twelve requested instruction in prayer.
Mark 6:41; John 6:11	Prayed before feeding the 5,000.
John 11:41,42	Prayed at the tomb of Lazarus, then called him from the dead!
Mark 1:35	Went out alone to an uninhabited area in the wee hours of the morning for there was no other "free time" for prayer.
Mark 6:46	Sent the twelve out to cross the Sea of Galilee to leave Him alone in the mountain to pray.
Mark 8:6	Prayed before feeding the 4,000.
Mark 9:29	His prayer relationship with His Father gave Him the power to heal terrible illnesses.
Mark 10:16	Jesus responded to mothers' desire for Him to pray for their children by taking them in His arms and blessing them.
Luke 10:21,22 Matthew 11:25-27	Jesus shared His joy with His Father in thanksgiving.

John 12:27,28	Prayed in soul unrest concerning the cross.

THE UPPER ROOM

Matthew 26:26,27	Gave thanks before sharing the Passover observance.
Luke 22:31,32	Told Peter that He had prayed for his faith to hold up under the coming stress.
John 14:13,14	Anything is ours if we ask in His name.
John 15:7-16	He repeats the promise of prayer's fulfillment.
John 16:23,24	Again, He emphasizes hope in prayer.
John 14:16; 16:26	When we pray in His name, He speaks to God for us.

THE GARDEN

John 17	Jesus' most complete recorded prayer.
John 18:1,2	The Garden was a much frequented place of prayer for Jesus.
Matthew 26:36-46 Mark 14:32-42 Luke 22:39-46	His agony in prayer.

ON THE CROSS

Luke 23:34	Amazing love!
Matthew 27:46 Mark 15:34	The depths He suffered for us as He became sacrifice for our sin.
Luke 23:46	The victorious cry of triumphal obedience.

AFTER THE RESURRECTION

Luke 24:30	Gave thanks at supper with disciples on road to Emmaus.
Luke 24:51	As He ascended, He was blessing the twelve. What a wonderful memory to encourage them.

Dear Friend:

I just had to send a note to tell you how much I love you and care for you.

I saw you yesterday as you were talking to your friend. I waited all day hoping you would want to talk with me. As evening came, I gave you a sunset to close your day and a breeze to rest you — and I waited. You never came. Sure, it hurts me — but I still love you because I am your friend.

I saw you fall asleep last night and longed to touch you, so I spilled moonlight on your face. Again I waited wanting to rush down so we could talk. I have so many gifts for you! You got up late and rushed off to work. My tears were in the rain.

Today you looked so sad — so all alone. It made my heart ache because I understand. My friends let me down and hurt me many times too, but I love them.

If you would only listen to me! I LOVE YOU! I try to tell you in the blue sky and in the quiet green grass. I whisper it in the leaves in the trees and breathe it in the color of flowers. I shout it to you in the mountain streams and give the birds love songs to sing. I clothe you with warm sunshine and sweeten the air with nature scents. My LOVE for you is deeper than the ocean and bigger than the biggest want or need in your head. If you only knew how much I want to talk and walk with you.

I know how hard it is on earth. I really know! and I want to help you. I want you to meet my father. He wants to help you too. My father is that way you know.

Just call me — ask me — talk with me! Please don't forget me! I have so much to share with you!

Alright, okay, I won't bother you any more. YOU are free to choose me. It's your decision. I have chosen you, and because of this, I will wait, and wait, and wait, because....I LOVE YOU.

Your friend,
JESUS

(Reprinted from LOVE LOGUE, a newsletter of Shore Community, New Jersey Marriage Encounter....February '79).

PRAYER THOUGHTS

O Lord, Thou knowest how busy I must be this day. If I forget thee, do not Thou forget me.   —Jacob Astley—

Lord, teach us to pray.   —Luke 11:1—

Be pleased, O Lord, to remember my friends, all that have prayed for me, and all that have done me good.

Do Thou good to them and return all their kindnesses double in their own bosom, sanctifying them with Thy graces, and bringing them to glory.

Let all my family and kindred, my neighbors and acquaintances receive the benefit of my prayers, and the blessings of God; in the comforts and supports of Thy providence, and the sanctification of Thy spirit.   —Jeremy Taylor—

O Lord, Thou lover of souls, in whose hand is the life of every living thing, we bring before Thee in our prayers all those who are lonely in the world. Thine they are, and none can pluck them out of Thy hand. In Thy pitying mercy let our remembrance reach them and comfort their hearts. For Thy love's sake...Amen.   —Anonymous—

Give me work
Till my life shall end
And life
Till my work is done.   —Yorkshire tombstone—

O Father, light up the small duties of this day's life: may they shine with the beauty of Thy countenance. May we believe that glory can dwell in the commonest task of every day.
    —St. Augustine—

Teach us, good Lord, to serve Thee as Thou deservest; to give and not to count the cost; to fight and not to heed the wounds; to toil and not to seek rest; to labor and not to ask for any reward; save that of knowing that we do Thy will.
    —Ignatius Loyola—

I thank Thee, Lord, for knowing me better than I know myself, and for letting me know myself better than others know me. Make me, I pray Thee, better than they suppose, and forgive me what they do not know.

    —Arabian—

O Lord our God, when the storm is loud, and the night is dark, and the soul is sad, and the heart oppressed; then as weary travelers, may we look to Thee; and beholding the light of Thy love, may it bear us on, until we learn to sing Thy song in the night.

—George Dawson—

O Lord, who art as a shadow of a great rock in a weary land, who beholdest Thy weak creatures, weary of labor, weary of pleasure, weary of hope deferred, weary of self, in Thine abundant compassion and unutterable tenderness, bring us unto Thy rest.

—Christina Rossetti—

O God, animate us to cheerfulness. May we have a joyful sense of our blessings, learn to look on the bright circumstances of our lot, and maintain a perpetual contentedness. Preserve us from despondency and from yielding to dejection. Teach us that nothing can hurt us if, with true loyalty and affection, we keep Thy commandments and take refuge in Thee.

—William E. Channing—

Father, let me hold Thy hand and like a child walk with Thee down all my days, secure in Thy love and strength.

—Thomas a'Kempis—

Lord, behold our family here assembled. We thank Thee for this place in which we dwell; for the love that unites us; for the peace accorded us this day; for the hope with which we expect the morrow; for the health, the work, the food and the bright skies that make our lives delightful; for our friends in all parts of the earth.

—Robert Louis Stevenson—

Let me not seek out of Thee what I can find only in Thee, O Lord, peace and rest and joy and bliss, which abide only in Thy abiding joy. Lift up my soul above the weary round of harassing thoughts to Thy eternal presence. Lift up my soul to the pure, bright, serene, radiant atmosphere of Thy presence, that there I may breathe freely, there repose in Thy love, there be at rest from myself, and from all things that weary me; and thence return, arrayed with Thy peace, to do and bear what shall please Thee.

—E. B. Pusey—

"More things are wrought by prayer than this world dreams of."

PRAYER FOR ANIMALS

Hear our humble prayer, O God,
For our friends the animals,
Especially for animals, who are suffering;
Or any that are hunted,
Or lost,
Or deserted,
Or frightened,
Or hungry;
For all that must be put to death.
We entreat for them all Thy mercy and pity,
And for all who deal with them
We ask a heart of compassion and gentle hands
and kindly words.
Make us ourselves to be true friends to animals
And so to enjoy the blessings of the merciful.

Table of Contents

PART I—POSITIVE, CREATIVE STEPS

PART II—LOOKING INWARD

PART III—MY PRAYERS FOR THOSE I LOVE BEST

PART IV – GOD'S FAMILY AND MY HEART

PART V – LIVING WITH MY FATHER

PART I
Positive Creative Steps

Prayer is reaching up with my heart.

CHAPTER 1

Increasing My Awareness of God

Prayer, the great, neglected privilege of imperfect, sinful humans from a loving perfect God.

Prayer, the conversation between two who love each other, child and heavenly Father.

Prayer, the struggling human cry for help to the omnipotent Redeemer.

Don't you agree that a shared study of prayer should begin with a prayer by those who are together reaching Godward for greater understanding of our blessings in prayer, and greater maturity in our relationship with God?

Holy Father, We bless Your dear Name, and praise You for Your goodness. We share a need for prayer in our lives. We want to live closer to You, to be a clearer reflection of Jesus' example. Some of us feel spiritually threadbare — we are worn out and pulled apart by pressures. Some of us are spiritually cold — our fires are flickering low and we are hoping for warmth. Some of us are happy — we are at peace and seek deeper delights in You. Some of us have an inner, private desperation, almost a silent hysterical screaming for help to deal with a situation because there is no one but You to rescue us, to show us a solution.

Some of us are standing at a crisis place and we are reaching for answers to a decision we cannot avoid. Some of us feel weak and long for renewal of our inner strength to be better able to serve as Jesus did. Some of us are on a spiritual plateau and need guidance from somewhere, from someone, to set us climbing and growing again. Father, hear each heart's cry and move with power to lead us to Your will in our personal circumstances.

Father, while we study, would You help us to let go of any distractions and trust You to care for the progress of the world without our concern? Increase our security in the knowledge that You love those who are dearest to us even more than we do. Let our minds be still, at rest, free of the burdens of yesterday, next week, and any immediate responsibilities and duties. Open our hearts to Your influence on our lives, to Your power to change us into responsive instruments singing Your song to a listening world. Help us to be truly thankful for our precious privilege of knowing You. In the dear name of Jesus, the Lord of our lives, Amen.

Beloved, we share an interest in prayer, because not one of us feels our prayer life is all that it could be, or certainly all that it should be. We know that prayer is a discipline, an art that is polished by practice, and we long for signposts to point us toward ways to make our prayers more effective and meaningful. We refuse to be frustrated or discouraged by knowing that on earth we can never completely perfect our prayer relationship to the Father because it grows deeper as the days, and months, and years go by. We identify with each other as we approach the study of prayer, for we are sisters in a family, loving the same Father, and following the same Lord.

Jesus A Man of Prayer

The desire of our hearts is to be like our Master, a man of prayer. Jesus began His ministry with prayer (Luke 3:21) and ended it with prayer (Luke 23:46). He lived and died in constant communication with His Father. He lived the loveliest of lives to give us a pattern to follow, "he that saith he abides in him ought himself to walk even as he walked" (1 John 2:6). Jesus lived a God-directed life, *perfectly* lived a God-directed life. As the Master teacher, He knew that it is much easier to learn a skill if we can see someone doing what we are expected to do. We can tell someone how to prepare a souffle, or blindstitch a hem, but it is much more helpful for her to watch us than it is to only hear our instruction. Jesus understands and reaches out to us with encouragement through His example to help us to see the character in action into whose likeness we are to grow, "till we all attain unto the unity of the faith, and of the knowledge of the Son of God, unto a fullgrown man, unto the measure of the stature of the fulness of Christ" (Ephesians 4:13). And a part of that fulness, of that example, was His prayer life.

Once, Jesus was a guest in Peter and Andrew's house as Mark records, "And in the morning, a great while before day, he rose up and went out, and departed into a desert place, and there prayed" (Mark 1:35). If you had an overnight guest, would you consider this strange behavior? Why did Jesus feel such a need for private communication with His Father so pressing that He would rise "a great while before day" and look for a quiet place away from people? The verses that precede Mark 1:35 describe the pressure of demands on Jesus for healing, for teaching by people who needed Him. He was constantly giving of Himself, draining His energy, patience, and stamina. Prayer was His renewal time, when the serenity, the peace, the strength of God rebuilt His inner self. He, the perfect Son of God, felt it a necessity to find, to plan, personal undisturbed time with His Father. This was His secret for keeping His relationships to those around Him balanced, and patient, and self-giving.

Jesus Brought Us a New Relationship to God

Wives and mothers know the empty feeling when even one day draws to a close and we have given our hearts and strengths in patient caring for the needs and problems of a family and there has not been one of them to refill our cup. How blessed we are as Christian women to have a Savior who knew the same emptiness! And, He showed us the way to keep on giving without feeling ourselves martyrs: a vital prayer life. He revealed a Father much more willing to have us come to Him than we are willing to pray.

Jesus had a "vertizontal" relationship; through reverent, personal communication with God and obedience to His will (the vertical relationship), He was able to reach out to meet the needs of all of those around Him (the horizontal relationship). When two relationships are explained in one word, we can borrow the coined expression, "vertizontal". The sign for our word would be a cross, the symbol of Jesus' perfection, for a horizontal line laid on top of a vertical line forms a cross.

It is only when our "vertizontal" relationships are balanced that we can approach the poise and self-giving of Jesus. If sin stands between us and our Father, we can't be happy or creative. If a store clerk is rude to us, or a child rebelliously tries our wits and patience, or a husband is upset with us, we cannot function with energy and optimism. The Jews have a word that expresses the vertizontally-balanced condition. It is shalom. We think of the translation of shalom as "peace". Shalom, to the Jew, is a wish for peace, but in an expanded meaining that includes everything that makes for a person's highest good. Notice shalom is not a wish for the absence of war or troubles, it is a wish for the presence of all good things. It is in the example of Jesus practiced day by day in our lives that we have peace, for the prophecy of Him was, "And this man shall be our peace" (Micah 5:5). This man, this Jesus is our peace. Knowing Him, loving Him, obeying Him, following His example, brings us peace — not the absence of trouble, but the presence of everything that makes life good, fulfilling and happy. He pointed the way to the discovery of that quality of life by leading us to see the inexpressible value of prayer as a vital, integral part of every day as natural and necessary as breathing or eating, or drinking.

Delighting in God

Jesus spoke in His prayer times not to an angry god who must be appeased or a cruel god who would crush people on a whim. Jesus spoke with His Father. When Dr. Luke writes of Jesus' great joy at the return of the seventy (Luke 10:21,22), he tells us that He turned to His Father in thanksgiving to share that joy. Isn't it true for us too, that we can't really enjoy the special delights in our lives unless we can share them with someone we love? Jesus turned to His Father. What an example for us!

Do we think of God as our Father who enjoys whatever makes us happy, a Father who *wants* to share those joys with us? Sadly, we think more often of His mercy, and compassion, and wisdom, and lean on Him in prayer for those graces in our hours of need. Here could be a new shared interest to develop in our prayers. Then, taking it one step further, we can learn to delight in God Himself, in His goodness, His blessings, the privilege of being welcome in His Presence. David wrote some very positive thoughts for our study concerning adoring God in joy:

> "Trust in Jehovah, and do good;
> Dwell in the land, and feed on his
> faithfulness.
> Delight thyself also in Jehovah;

4

> And he will give thee the desires of
> thy heart.
> Commit thy way unto Jehovah;
> Trust also in him, and he will
> bring it to pass.
> And he will make thy righteousness
> go forth as the light,
> And thy justice as the noon-day.
> Rest in Jehovah and wait patiently
> for him........"Psalm 37:3-7A

Look carefully for the promise to those who delight in the Father. To delight in Him would include being aware of Him, quiet time shared with Him, *knowing Him.* One of the blessings in a study of prayer is a restored, widened and deepened delight in God, and in those who also love Him.

For the Seeker

1. Which of the following words most accurately describe my relationship with God?

guarded	reserved for crisis times
open ✓	warm, loving ✓
stiff	fearful
expectant of good	not as I want it to be
dull, lifeless	cautious
close ✓	vague
supportive ✓	adoring ✓
vital	awkward
haphazard	reverently comfortable ✓

others? _____

2. Write a brief paragraph using the words you selected above to express your evaluation of your relationship to God as you see it now, at this point in time. On a scale of 1-10, where are you with regard to your highest goal? *Open, close, suppor-*
tive, warm, loving, adoring,
reverently comfortable 9
_____

3. Prayer, or worded communion, is only one segment of our relationship to God. Jesus was perfect, balanced in every relationship, vertizontally balanced. He had the perfection of inner con-
formity to Galatians 5:22,23 that expressed itself in quiet dignity,
self-forgetfulness, and the ability to give of Himself to others
beyond human expectation (Mark 3:20,21).

From a study of the Scriptures used in Chapter 1, what was the
importance of Jesus' prayer life in living the lovely life He did as
our example? __He had the faith, and__
__he had Knowledge__

4. Is there someone I love that delights me, that lights up my life?
What had to occur before I could delight in him/her? How could I
transfer this insight to my relationship with God? _____

5. Suggested memory work:
   1 John 2:5,6
   Psalm 37:3-7A

6

CHAPTER 2

I Know I Should Pray More....
I Wonder Why I Don't

Prayer is reaching up with our hearts.
Prayer is overcoming a feeling of worthlessness to cry out to God
anyway.
Prayer is training myself to respond to life around me by placing
the whole of it in the loving, wise hands of my Father.

Each of us has been puzzled at times in our walk with God by the
thought, "I know I should pray more......I wonder why I don't?" Our
stumbling block to enjoying God, and to being open with Him in prayer,
could be that, without realizing it, we judge Him by the way people respond to us. If our earthly fathers made us feel unimportant, if they had
no time for us, if our husbands were not able to communicate warmth to
us, then we unconsciously assume that God is the same in response.
We cannot allow ourselves to blame God for what people do to us.
Have you ever thought, "I won't bother God with this, it isn't important
enough", or "I'm not important — God wouldn't want to hear from
me?" As women, we still carry with us the deep yearnings we felt as girls
for our Dads to have warm, loving, meaningful communication with us.
    Young people, and adults, equate being listened to, attentively and
sympathetically, with being loved. Jesus spoke to our need to know His
Father as He really is; listen to Jesus, "If you, then, though you are evil,
know how to give good gifts to your children, how much more will your
Father in heaven give good gifts to those who ask Him" (Matthew 7:11
NIV). Perhaps we have few blessings because we fail to ask?

7

God's Concern For His Own

On another occasion, Jesus spoke of the detailed care of God for His own, "And be not afraid of them that kill the body, but are not able to kill the soul: but rather fear him who is able to destroy both soul and body in hell. Are not two sparrows sold for a penny? and not one of them shall fall on the ground without you Father: but the very hairs of your head are all numbered. Fear not, therefore: ye are of more value than many sparrows" (Matthew 10:28-31). Oh! The good news of Jesus' message! The Jews who heard Him speak knew well His illustration about the sparrows and probably were astonished by it. For you see, a sparrow was the cheapest of the acceptable sacrificial creatures that could be offered by the poor. Two sparrows could be purchased for a penny. In a parallel account in Luke 12:6, he tells us that if a person was willing to spend two pennies, he could buy *five* sparrows. The extra one was added as having no value at all. God cares for sparrows — His infinite love toward creation! Such a teaching would have been an amazing thought to the people of that culture. They would have found it incredible that God noticed even the forgotten, valueless sparrow! Yet the Master assures us that not one of them can light on the ground without his Father's watchful care. How many times a day does one sparrow light on the ground? Jesus goes on connecting the thought of God's concern for the sparrow with the hairs of our heads. How many hairs do you have on your head? How many did you clean from your brush and comb this morning? God knows. God's love is so all encompassing that there is no detail of our lives that goes without His notice, no place inaccessible to His Presence, no time inconvenient for His attention to our needs. Thank you, Father.

Father-Hunger

The results of a recent survey among children ages nine through twelve might help us to see our personal barriers between us and the Father. These children responded to questions about their relationships with their dads, and the results are alarming: 1. They don't confide their secrets to their fathers. 2. They prefer television to their dads. 3. The person they most feared was their dads. 4. The person who gives them the least time, attention and affection in the family is their dad. The conclusion: mothers are blamed for the problems that children have, but it seems that *father-hunger* is the larger cause. Can we identify with any of their responses? Does this speak to the state of neglect our prayer life suffers? We must believe in our worth before God, and in His love for us, before we can be eager to pray. The failure of communication between a child and her dad could be brought about by his demonstrated disinterest in her conversation. Listening is a shared responsibility between the person speaking and the person listening. And if the listener doesn't show genuine interest and sensitivity to what is being said, the speaker will stop talking, and the communication will fail.

Satisfying Father-Hunger

Jesus says that God, the perfect Father, has genuine interest and sensitivity to what we say, and do, and yearn for, and suffer with. If we believe this, we lose our reluctance to pray. A shared study of prayer allows us the grand opportunity to listen to each other and to learn from each other in love as we reaffirm our value to our heavenly Father. And, as we do this, the Psalmist's words will come alive in our hearts, "As the deer pants for the streams of water, so my soul pants for you, O God. My soul thirsts for God, for the living God. When can I go and meet with God? By day the Lord directs his love, at night his song is with me — a prayer to the God of my life" (Psalm 42:1,2,8 NIV).

Wouldn't it be marvelous to be able to "pray without ceasing" (1 Thessalonians 5:17) or to pray all night as Jesus did? (Luke 6:12). We have interruptions, duties to fulfill, demands for our attention and our time. In worship, mothers must even learn to pray in interrupted concentration because of the precious, squirming, restless child that she is loving into loving God. Is there ever a time in life more than any other when it is easier to find the uncluttered quiet time to pray? Not really. There are plans, pressures, aches and pains, duties, interruptions, things to do, people to see, at any age.

Raising the Percentage of Time Spent in Prayer

How then can we raise our percentage of time spent in prayer? How can we become more conscious of His Presence with us moment by moment? What are some signposts directing us Godward in developing our prayer lives? Sometimes in keeping our active schedules, we feel we should pray as a British general, Jacob Astley, once prayed before a battle, "O Lord, Thou knowest how busy I must be this day. If I forget Thee, do not Thou forget me". The power to assist us in working toward our goals is here in our shared yearning, our combined desire to grow in communication with the Father, "Again I say unto you that if two of you shall agree on earth as touching anything that they shall ask, it shall be done for them of My Father who is in heaven. For where two or three or gathered together in My Name, there am I in the midst of them" (Matthew 18:19,20).

What would your personal estimate be of the percentage of time you are conscious of God's presence or in prayer? Keep that percentage number in you heart as a measuring mark from which to chart your progress.

Let's consider some practical, although elementary, signposts to remind us of prayer and turn us to God. We could call these "over the shoulder" prayers. David prayed this way running for his life from his son, Absalom. "And David went up by the ascent of the mount of Olives, and wept as he went up; and he had his head covered, and went barefoot: and all the people that were with him covered every man his head, and they went up, weeping as they went up. And one told David, saying, Ahithophel is among the conspirators with Absalom. And David said, O Jehovah, I pray thee, turn the counsel of Ahithophel into foolishness" (2 Samuel 15:30,31). It was a heartbreaking, panic-filled hour for David. He had no time to bow in formal prayer. He made a sincere plea as it were "over his shoulder". The blessing for us is the good news that David's hurried prayer was answered! "And Absolom and all the men of Israel said, The counsel of Hushai the Archite is better than the counsel of Ahithophel, to the intent that Jehovah might bring evil on Absalom" (2 Samuel 17:14). God can work mightily with bits and pieces of prayer we offer Him even in haste.

We can train ourselves to respond with prayer to life around us. Prayer is in part a discipline like jogging, or parenting, or dieting, or typing, in that we are conscious of a need and then work to fill the need.

Signals For Prayer

Here are some suggested signposts and ideas for "over the shoulder" prayers.

1. Any school building — Be with all those who are struggling to learn. Be with those who feel left out of the group. Be with the teachers and grant them patience and understanding.

2. Any clinic or hospital — Be with those who are dying or in pain, and with those who love them. Be with the nurses who are tired and pressured by responsibility. Grant the doctors wisdom and gentle hands. Bless the women in labor and the babies in the

10

nursery. Let the little ones go home to welcoming arms.

3. Rude clerks or waitresses — Help me to smile and wish them only good. Perhaps You will work through me to change their day.

4. When the telephone rings — Speak through me, Lord. Guard my tongue. Bless the caller.

5. Passing or hearing an ambulance — Be with the sufferer and the ones who minister to her needs. Thank you for my health.

6. Clocks/Watch — There is no reason You should allow me this day. Thank You for Your grace. Help me to use time for Your glory and to serve Your purpose for my life here.

7. Passing a police car — Protect this officer from harm today. Bless him as a guardian of peace. Help wrongdoers to repent and find a better way to live. (Or quote a hymn, "Those who plan some evil, from their sin restrain").

8. Introductions — If I can touch Mary Jones with Your love, please use me, Father. Help her to feel important to You.

One sentence is usually a good "over the shoulder" prayer. Discard these ideas for your own better ideas, or use them with your own additions to the signposts. We need reminders to call us to God's nearness.

Some people prefer to use 'Thee' and 'Thou' instead of 'You' and that is fine. Use whatever language you feel the most comfortably reverent with in speaking to the Father. Jesus spoke to Him in the language spoken by those around Him. We don't speak Aramaic, or Greek, or Hebrew, so most of us employ the language spoken by those with whom we live.

Developing My Personal Prayer Life

This study is planned as a vehicle for developing your personal prayer life from wherever you are now to another level, closer to where you would like to be in your relationship to the Father. The progress will be accomplished by your own seeking, and studying, and then applying your discoveries in prayer.

If you are sharing this study with a ladies' group or retreat, the workshop times will be moments of sharing, encouragement, strengthening, and supportive love from your sisters. There are assignments to work through with your group, followed by a period of silence for you to be alone with the Father. A hymn will call you back to rejoin your group.

If you are working on the study alone, you could set a timer to remind you of the close of your silent time in order to release you from the distraction of clock-watching, freeing you to be more sensitively tuned to spiritual concerns.

It is a one on one encounter when we each in our hearts' solitude commit ourselves to communication with the Father. There we find no cheering crowds of supporters, no bands to encourage, no victory shouts of "You're number one!" It is a relationship that blesses a hundred-fold the persevering, dedicated seeker who refuses to be discouraged. Prayer can change us as we learn to hear God's guidance, to surrender to His will. The joys are deeper and ever deeper to those adventurous souls who are willing to yield their hearts, and minds, and energies to the neglected privilege of prayer.

Why is it that the exalted honor of communicating with the Almighty Creator God who controls all things is easily pushed aside and forgotten in our busy lives? Would we thrill more if we held a moon-rock in our hands than we do to the awesome realization of God's Presence and loving concern constantly with us?

For the Seeker

1. Do you agree with the author's statement, "Young people, and adults, equate being listened to, attentively and sympathetically, with being loved"? If so, from God's point of view, do I love Him by attentively and sympathetically listening to Him? Write out in your own words what you think God is saying to you personally about Himself in Matthew 10:28-31. _____
   _____
   _____
   _____

2. Can I identify my personal barriers to a meaningful prayer life?
   Too busy
   I don't have time because I don't plan time.
   If He knows everything, He doesn't need me to talk to Him.
   I don't have anything important enough to say to bother Him with it.
   I'm embarrassed to face Him because He knows the real me, my sins, my faults, my failures, my inadequacies, my secret heart.

I'm not ready to surrender my will to His.

I'm not sure I'm ready to let Him move close to me and then adjust to the changes that follow.

Do these statements help you to probe for your own reasons/excuses for the weaknesses in your prayer life? _____

_____

_____

_____

3. Do I believe, devoutly affirm that the Father has genuine interest in what I say, and do, and yearn for, and suffer with, and find joy in? Read Psalm 139:1-18 and list the different ways David expresses God's personal concern for you.

      GOD'S CONCERN   VERSE

_____

_____

_____

_____

_____

4. Suggested memory work:
      Matthew 7:11
      Matthew 10:28-31
      Psalm 42:1,2,8
      Matthew 18:19,20

Prayer Workshop Time I

To me, prayer is _____

_____

How long have I been a Christian?

List as many personal blessings as you can in five minutes. Choose your favorite five to share.

For the silent time to follow, each lady can remain where she is or move to some other room/area she chooses.

Silent Hour Meditation Questions (Suggested time length: 15 minutes)

Do I pray......often?......sometimes?......at least once a day?......only at/never at mealtime?

Do I now, totally and completely as I am able to at this point in my life, give myself to God and place myself under His management?
If I am not willing to give myself totally and completely as I can, why am I balking at surrender? How much of myself am I willing to release to Him?

What new areas of my life can I give to Him?

Do I *practice* the theology expressed in James 5:13? (Might memorize this verse and use it in life).

Suggested activity: read some of the prayers quoted in the book, or read the scriptures listed relating Jesus' teachings on prayer and His prayer life.
Memorize one of His teachings on prayer with the reference. Let the words become your only conscious thoughts. Leave God room to enrich them with fresh insight and meaning specifically for your needs or to bless another.
"For this cause I bow my knees to the Father, from whom every family in heaven and on earth is named, that He would grant you, according to the riches of His glory, that ye may be strengthened with power through His Spirit in the inward man" (Ephesians 3:14-16).
The silent times are most effective if *all verbal* communication is suspended.
If the study is a group-sharing rather than a personal study, let one person be assigned to watch the time, and to call the group back together with a hymn the ladies can join as they make their way back to their sharing groups. If you are using this book for a private study, you could set the timer on your stove to free you from watching the time while you meditate.

Group Discussion Or Thought Questions to Summarize Part I

Did you feel comfortable in a planned time of prayer?

How did you respond to the use of the time? Prayer only, prayer and reading, etc.

Would you share any insight you gained? If too personal to share, please write it out because it is amazing how quickly it is forgotten in rapid growth. This is one of your milestones on the upward climb closer to the will and heart of God. _____

_____

_____

_____

_____

Think a little more about "over the shoulder" prayers — our first signposts reminders:

> ambulance
> irritable clerk/waitress
> watch
> ringing telephone
> introductions
> newscasts
> police car
> hospital
> school
> first thought on awakening *before* you get
> out of bed in the morning

Could you share a scripture verse for each/any of these situations? Use a concordance if you need to locate a verse.

PART II
Looking Inward

A concept of Jesus' mediator relationship in my prayer life.

CHAPTER 3

It's Me, O Lord, Standing in the Need of Prayer

Prayer is our response to the goodness of God.

Prayer is letting God into our lives.

Prayer is putting God in touch with us.

"For where two or three are gathered together in My Name, there am I in the midst of them" (Matthew 18:20). There is our power to grow — the Christ with us! What a promise! How good the Father is!

Our Bibles Are a Treasure-House of Prayer

The gospel writers present Jesus in His earthly life as a Man of prayer. If you would like to see prayer blossom like Easter lilies when you turn the pages of your Bible, begin in the gospels with a colored pen and underline all the references to prayer, all the prayers, — anywhere the words pray or prayer are found. Green seems an appropriate color, restful, relaxed, calm yet vibrant with the hue of living plants. It is a thrilling new dimension to your study when you can see the verses leap out from the pages to arrest your attention. Perhaps you will continue through the New Testament and re-read the Old Testament to discover prayer references there. Don't miss the treasures hidden for the seeker's delight.

Jesus the Perfect Mediator

Think about your written response when you completed your sentence, "Prayer is.....". On the small child's level, we teach that prayer is "talking to God". That concept hardly satisfies the more mature Christian's needs. It falls short of the concept of prayer we observe in our Master as revealed in the gospels, or of His involvement with and for us now, doesn't it? In 1 Timothy 2:5 we find these words, "For there is one God, one mediator also between God and men, himself man, Christ Jesus". Jesus has a vertizontal relationship now too, He horizontally takes us by the hand, and vertically represents us before the Father.

He is our Mediator. What does a mediator do? What are the qualities of a mediator? He is a middleman with the foremost function of bringing God and man together. Jesus is the perfect mediator because He can represent us to God remembering His days in the flesh for He was human, and He can represent God to us for Jesus is Divine! There is only one mediator between God and us because Jesus is the only person in eternity or time that has been both human and divine.

Let's go a bit further in our understanding of Jesus as our mediator. A mediator has the duty of establishing communication between two parties, or groups, who are in dispute. Now in the case of Jesus' mediation, His task is not to establish the communication between God and us, for God does not need reconciling to us. He has always yearned after us. His book is a record of His love for us, and our total misunderstanding of Him. Jesus' work as mediator then is to bring us to God in a manner that would cause us to hate our sins, to turn us to a loving Father for grace and mercy instead of our futilely attempting to hide or to run away from Him.

If a mediator restores communication in the spiritual realm, Jesus establishes communciation between God and us. Prayer becomes both speaking and listening, a dialogue and not a soliloquy. We must be careful not to do all the talking. Prayer is definitely not placing words before God, leaving them and quickly turning to other duties. Prayer is time spent with the reverent courtesy from us of listening as well as speaking. Prayer is letting God into the core, the center of our being. More than letting Him in, prayer is welcoming Him in. What a pleasure, a blessing, to be with Someone from whom there is no need to hide anything, with Someone who knows us exactly as we are for He made us, and best of all, with Someone who loves us, and *accepts* us just the way we are! You see, Jesus goes far beyond establishing communication (wonderful as that is); He has brought about a personal, enduring relationship between daughters and a Father. The bond that draws us together is the bond of love. God is love (1 John 4:8,16), so He needs us — for love must have someone to love. We are weak, helpless, sinful, so we need God, "for all have sinned, and fallen short of the glory of God" (Romans 3:23); our dear Savior, is the middleman, the

Mediator, who stands between God and us, drawing us, lifting us closer and closer to God.

Jesus Showed Us The Father

Jesus came to let us know who God is and what the Father is really like. We might use the illustration of the visitor on a White House tour. The person has read the words of the President, seen him on television, heard his voice, but lacks a personal knowledge of the man. Suppose the visitor is singled out for the honor of walking through the private presidential quarters and personally spending time with the President.

Would the visitor have a better understanding of the man then? God has through the centuries since creation revealed Himself to mankind in words, visions, through prophets, patriarchs, poets and in patience beyond our understanding; still people could not comprehend the truths before them until Jesus came. Jesus was Divinity in flesh who spoke as we speak, felt as we feel, was tried as we are tried. He told His disciples that last night before the cross, "He that hath seen me, hath seen the Father" (John 14:9). Notice what Jesus does not say, "He that hath seen Me, hath seen God". Not hath seen God, but hath seen the *Father*. In prayer we approach a *Father*, a heavenly Father who is a perfect Father, unlimited in love,
> unlimited in creativity,
> unlimited in power,
> unlimited in wisdom,
> unlimited in time to listen to us,
> unlimited in tender care for our needs.

Jesus showed us a Father who responded in understanding love to the lonely, penitent prostitute, who touched the decaying leper, who gave of Himself to the sick, who loved and gently handled little children. God is like that.

Jesus in His pressured earthly ministry, never turned anyone away because He would have been inconvenienced. God is like that.

God is Looking For Us

God is more eager to hear us pray than we are to pray. Jesus brought the good news that God is seeking worshippers, "But the hour cometh, and now is when the true worshippers shall worship the Father in spirit and truth: for such doth the Father seek to be his worshippers" (John 4:23).

Living With My Father

God is looking for us! Jesus told us about, showed us, a Father who loves us more than we can understand — perhaps even in eternity. How many of us treat Him as our teens react to us because they fail to understand our love includes an interest in their lives that enjoys sharing anything they do, anywhere they go, anyone they see? What is most often the response when a daughter is welcomed home by questions like:

Did you have a good time?

Who was there?

Did anyone compliment your new dress?

Most of us could sadly confess that we spend our lives, like the elder brother, not in a far country, not in rebellion, not in blatant sin, but in obedience without love, failing to communicate our longings to our Father, indifferently or unthinkingly shutting the Father out of our consciousness a greater part of the time (Luke 15:25-31).

Our study is an expression of a need, of a yearning to increase the percentage of time we consciously spend with the Father. We want Him to be the Person we would most like to spend time with. We want to share our lives with Him as His beloved children.

For the Seeker

1. Our topic has been the personal need for prayer. Jesus demonstrated His need for prayer while He shared our "humanness". Paul requested the prayers of the Christians he loved and he prayed for them. Research as many references as you can where Paul prayed or requested prayers. _____

   _____

   _____

   _____

   _____

2. Read through the list of references of Paul's prayer life; put down the specific requests he asked people to pray for him. You are listing Paul's needs that he knew could be answered only by God.

   _____

   _____

   _____

   _____

3. Using your same reference, write down the things Paul prayed for himself. _____

_____
_____
_____

4. Does your study of Paul's prayer-life bring you insight of new dimensions you can explore in your own prayers? If so, what are the insights? _____

_____
_____
_____
_____

5. Do the thoughts discussed of Jesus as my Mediator lifting me ever nearer God's heart, encourage me to devote more conscious thought to being aware of His Presence? What feelings do I discover that are new to me in association with the idea of prayer? _____

_____
_____
_____
_____

6. The statement was made that prayer is communication between two, God and me. Perhaps you need some time to consider the concept? _____

_____
_____

Help Me, O Lord, To See Myself With Spiritually Sensitive Eyes

Prayer is enduring; inward, personal
 communion with God.
  Prayer is getting to the point
   with God.
    Prayer is listening for God's
     answer with quiet confidence.
What are some roadblocks to our desired walk with the Father? See if any of these responses from some Christian sisters lead you to find your own personal roadblocks:

 "I become so busy with necessary tasks that I forget to pray."
 "I have bitter resentment toward someone that I feel justified
 in having."
 "I'm unable to forgive someone a wrong done to me."
 "I carry grudges and then try to get even."
 "I feel if God truly loved me I wouldn't have suffered the
 heartache that I have."
 "Sometimes I realize I avoid prayer because I know I need to
 let go of a bad attitude, or change a plan, and I don't want
 to."

It is painful to root up the weeds that are choking out our prayer life. Surgery is painful too, but it saves lives. Go after those roadblocks and destroy them with the power of God in the Spirit's sword and travel on to the next test of your life in Him.

The Power in Us

How can our Mediator help us to find and eradicate our prayer roadblocks? We know that as Christians, we abide in Him. The word "Abide" in Greek carries the meaning: an enduring, inward, personal communion. John recorded this saying of Jesus, "If ye abide (have an enduring, inward, personal communion) in me, and my words abide (hold His words in an enduring, inward, personal communion) in you, ask whatsoever ye will, and it shall be done unto you" (John 15:7). His words in us lead to having a more effective, powerful prayer life. We want to learn to be in constant touch with the power of His word and with Jesus Himself living in us. How can we go about accomplishing this? Let me suggest two ways that might be helpful in discovering applications of John 15:7.

1. We can be more specific in prayer. The prayer, "Help me to be a better wife and mother" is a general prayer. "Help me to be more responsive sexually to my husband," or "Grant me the strength to be patient with my children and to really listen not only to their words but the unspoken cries of their hearts," are specific prayers. Specific sharing of a need with God is to let Him move into a situation.

2. When we are serious about our prayer lives, we spend more time with the word, learning from our Example and Teacher, and maturing in His likeness. Do you ever put marks in your Bible that are signposts to you? We discussed underlining prayer themes in green. You could try underlining reactions to Jesus in yellow ("they glorified God", "turned away sorrowfully") or His reactions to people ("Jesus wept", "he marvelled because of their unbelief"). Or read through the gospels noticing Jesus' foretelling of the cross, the plot against Him, the trials and crucifixion, underlining these passages in red. Each area of interest you search out and fit together will broaden your concept of God Himself and the perfect way His plans are carried out, and will build your faith. If underlining is not appealing to you, you might consider using symbols in the margin as a signpost. A star could mean: this passage said something very important to me, or a cross could mean: I need to pray about this and work on it in my life. Be creative in your approach to the Word and find God's message for you, a vital part of your personal communication with Him.

Lurking Selfishness, A Formidable Barrier

It could be that the most disturbing, distracting, difficult-to-see-in-ourselves roadblock to prayer is the weakness, the sin of selfishness. "Ye lust, and have not: ye kill, and covet, and cannot obtain: ye fight and war; ye have not because ye ask not. Ye ask and receive not, because ye ask amiss, that ye may spend it on your pleasures" (James 4:2,3). Selfishness blinds us to our own sin. We cannot be God-centered and self-centered at the same time. Jeremiah wrote, "The heart is deceitful above all things, and it is exceedingly corrupt: who can know it?" (Jeremiah 17:9). With our rationalizations and excuses to ourselves for personal sins, we are easily deceived and cannot clearly excise them from our lives. It seems that on every threshold of spiritual growth there stands the Devil with selfishness to ruin our prayer of praise. For example, you pray to be the best teacher for five-year-olds that you can be. You work, study, make visual aids, attend workshops, and teach, teach, teach. Time passes and you are being recognized for your skill and ability. God answered your prayer. You feel good about this area of your service. Then a newcomer arrives to be part of the congregation and proves to be a better equipped, more advanced teacher for five-year-olds. Are you glad she came to teach you more than you know? Are you jealous of her spreading reputation? Had your desire to serve the Master subtly become a desire to be known? (Why is it no matter how well we do anything there will always be someone who does it better?) Selfishness is so near to each of us that the Devil has no difficulty using it to erect a barrier between us and our Father.

Unthankful Heart — Who Me?

The last roadblock we will consider together is the unthankful heart. Think about your prayers for the last week. Were the requests balanced by praise? Was there any thanksgiving at all? A void of praise and thanksgiving in prayer is the same as throwing away the key that unlocks the golden treasure chest of answers from God. Thanksgiving in prayer results in an inner peace the world cannot tear away from us, try as it will. "In nothing be anxious; but in everything by prayer and supplication with thanksgiving let your requests be made known unto

God. And the peace of God, which passeth all understanding, shall guard your hearts and your thoughts in Christ Jesus" (Philippians 4:6,7). Beloved, when we let thankfulness slip away from us, we become enslaved to worry. Worry is lack of faith, a lack of a prayerful response to life. Worry will strangle our prayer life! Thanksgiving, counting our blessings will open our eyes to God's tender care, and abundant providing, and our security in His wisdom and power.

God's Supportive Voice to Jesus in Times of Need

Was Jesus' prayer life different from ours in that He heard the very Voice of His Father as we would a counsellor across a desk from us? Yes, on the occasions of pressing need, of decision, the Voice was heard by others. At other times, Jesus must have prayed as we do with no Voice heard by the ear in response to his words or surely one of the gospel writers would have noted such an important fact.

Have you ever thought about the moments God's Voice came to Jesus? God spoke to Him at His baptism bringing Jesus confidence, support and reassurance at the beginning of His ministry (Luke 3:21,22). The Voice came again on the mountain when He was transfigured. Jesus had been praying, and Moses and Elijah came to speak with Him "about his decease which he was about to accomplish in Jerusalem" (Luke 9:28-31). Jesus had made His decision to give His physical life in the terrible ordeal of the cross, and the Voice came to strengthen Him and to reaffirm the love that was stronger than death. His divinity abhorred the prospect of becoming sin, separating Himself from His Father. His passion for doing God's will on earth as it is done in heaven battled His knowledge of the agony ahead. Jesus struggled with obedience, with nerving Himself to pay the price of being the Son of God.

Martyrs through the ages have gone to their deaths with strength beyond human resources surging in their hearts because they knew their Savior had shared their fears and conquered them, and in His power, they also died in triumph! John alone records the third occasion of God's Voice from heaven, "Now is my soul troubled; and what shall I say? Father, save me from this hour. But for this cause came I unto this hour. Father, glorify thy name. There came therefore a voice out of heaven, saying, I have both glorified it, and will glorify it again" (John 12:27,28). In answer to Jesus' tension, in reply to His prayerful agony to obey, the Father strengthens His son with supportive love, sustaining Jesus' resolve to endure by the reinforcement of His constant nearness and approval.

God Is There For Us Too

The Father is the same way today. He doesn't speak audibly from heaven, but He doesn't leave us to struggle without directions and guidance to complete a task He has given. The dialogue is there, "if My words abide in you". The God-breathed, living words, complete and perfect, are our power to live as God directs.

Beloved, the power for an intelligent, dynamic life of prayer is found in these verses from Romans 8, "And in like manner the Spirit also helpeth our infirmity; for we know not how to pray as we ought; but the Spirit Himself makes intercessions for us with groanings which cannot be uttered; and He that searches the hearts knows what is the mind of the Spirit, because He makes intercession for the saints according to the will of God" (Romans 8:26,27).

Those who are saints received the gift of the Spirit's Presence at our baptism (Acts 2:38). The Spirit came and settled down to take residence in our hearts (James 4:5). He is our seal that makes us as God's own in the world, as His people bound for heaven. He is our down payment, our guarantee of eternal life (Ephesians 1:13,14). He is just like Jesus. He is our friend sent by God to help us. He is the loving One who forms Jesus' character in us (John 14:16,17, 16:7-18; Galatians 5:16-18,22-25).

The Spirit is the power of our prayer lives. Verses 26 and 27 from Romans 8 speak to us of the loving Father's understanding that we would not know how to pray without help. We can't see the future, we don't know what our own real needs are, so how could we pray as wisely as we desire to? The word "helps" in the Greek is a picture word. It describes two who carry a burden between them. It is the same word Martha used when she complained to the Master about her sister (Luke 10:40). Martha meant, "Lord, ask Mary to come lend me a hand." The Spirit "lends us a hand" in our prayers and is an important part of our access to God. The Spirit doesn't change our words, but rather expresses our inarticulate longings to the Father. He can do this because He knows all we experience and understands us. He works for us as our attorney for the defense, presenting our case in ways of which we have no knowledge. In John 14:16,17, the Spirit is called our Comforter or

Paraclete with the Father. This role is the role Jesus filled Himself while on earth (Luke 22:31,32). Paraclete is a term representing a pleader who comes forward in favor of and representing another. The Spirit "pleads" from earth; Jesus "mediates" in heaven (Hebrews 7:25). As the Spirit shares our thoughts and understands us, He also shares God's thoughts and understands Him. The Spirit knows the will of God for us and leads us through the Word to be conformed ever closer to Jesus' character.

The lesson here for us is that if we expect to have a powerful, rich prayer life, we must lead lives that are yielded to the Lord. We need to walk in the way God planned for us, to do what God has for us to accomplish.

In the Spirit's care, we will live creatively, for in Him we have a Friend who has all the creativity of God, the Father, Himself!

Would you like to try an experiment? Set aside a definite time every day to read God's word and to pray. This is not a lesson preparation time, or a study time. It can be ten minutes, or more. You may need to set your alarm a bit earlier in order to be alone, but do find the time. Set a timer for the length of time you plan to spend. Read a selected passage of Scripture. You could have as a goal: reading through the New Testament, Psalms, or one gospel, whatever you select. Begin reading, concentrating on the words as you read, shutting out any other thoughts that intrude. When you find a new insight or thought, even if it is in the first verse you read, shut your Bible, close your eyes, relax and try to wipe your mind of everything. Make it a blank. See what God writes there. You might keep a personal record of your insights as you read. His voice, His guidance, His directives are there if we learn to hear them and study to know Him in His word.

God answers our prayers in many ways. We may find His message in the counsel of a husband or a friend. We may see it in the beauty of nature. We may hear it in the words of a loved hymn. We may look back on our lives and, because we unmistakably discern His providential care guiding our yesterdays, learn to endure today in confident faith that He is still with us while we wait for an answer. We may not receive exactly what we asked for, but we can be certain it is the very best answer, perfectly suited to our needs, so that we will more surely be prepared to enter heaven.

Let's learn to look to Jesus in expectant faith for answers to our seekings. He would say to us as He did to the blind men in the long ago, "According to your faith be it done unto you", and Matthew adds, "And their eyes were opened" (Matthew 9:29,30).

For the Seeker

1. Jesus did not do for people what they could do for themselves. For example: He raised Lazarus from the dead, but He had those in the crowd remove the boulder blocking the entrance to the tomb and take the grave clothes off the resurrected one. Let's apply this principle to eradicating the roadblocks in our prayer lives.

_____
_____
_____
_____

2. Do you agree with the statement that "His words in us lead to a more effective, powerful prayer life? If so, what step could you take toward having more of the word in your daily walk with the Savior? _____

_____
_____

3. Practice the instruction of Philippians 4:6,7 by pushing the worry into a smaller and smaller part of your prayers by offering more and more adoration and thanksgiving. List some of the attributes of God Himself worthy of adoration and precious to you. _____

_____
_____
_____

4. What have you thanked God for today? _____

_____

   What can you thank Him for now? _____

_____

5. Think about this quote: Worry is like a prayer to a false god. Does the truth of this statement somehow help you to recoil from worry? _____

_____

Prayer Workshop Time II

As with any study, you will need aids for research. It would be very helpful, even necessary, to have a concordance, a dictionary, a Nave's and several versions of the Scriptures (particularly the Amplified, Phillips and New International). Select a word or words from the "Word List" on the next page that you find uniquely speaks to your personal needs. (For a retreat, in the interest of time, it might be a good idea to limit yourself to one or two, no more than three words in order to concentrate effectively in a structured activity). Read through the Scripture verses relating to your word. Choose the verses that apply the most fittingly. If none of these verses meets your specific need, use a concordance, or the assistance of a fellow group member to select verses you find more suitable.

1. Write your word, then the Scripture verse with the reference.

2. Copy the definition of your word from the dictionary.

3. During the meditation time, use the Scripture verses to put you in touch with the Christ within you. Allow God to convict you with answers and guidance. Write out any additional verses that speak to your word.

Word List

Faith . . . . .1. John 5:13; Galatians 5:22; James 1:6-8; 2:14; Matthew 6:25-34; Mark 11:22-25

Doubt . . . . Luke 12:22-34; John 20:26-31; Matthew 14:29-33; Psalm 126; Romans 14:23

Humility . . . . . . James 4:6,10; Philippians 2:1-11; 1 Peter 5:6,7; Luke 18:9-14; Matthew 18:1-4; Matthew 5:3,5,6; Ephesians 5;21; 1 Corinthians 10:12; Romans 12:3,10,16; John 13:14-16; 1 Timothy 1:15; 1 Peter 3:2-4

Gratitude . . . . . Colossians 1:12,13; 1 Thessalonians 5:18; Hebrews 13;15; Ephesians 5:4,19,20; Philippians 4:4-7; Psalms 100; 116:12,14-19; 2 Corinthians 2:14

Knowledge . . . . John 4:39-42; 8:32; Hosea 4:6; Proverbs 1:7; 2 Peter 1:5-7; 3:18; 1 Peter 3:15; Hebrews5:11-6:1; 2 Timothy 3:14-17; 2:15; Matthew 7:7-11

Strength . . . . . . Isaiah 40:29-31; 41:10; Philippians 4:13,19; 2 Corinthians 12:8,9; Psalms 46:1,2; Proverbs 31:17; Ephesians 3:14-19; 6:10; Colossians 1:9-13; Hebrews 4:15,16; Psalm 138:3

Time . . . . John 9:4; Romans 13:11,12; Galatians 6:9; Ephesians 5:15-17; Colossians 4:5,6; Matthew 6:33; Hebrews 4:15,16; James 4:14,15; 1 Peter 1:13-21; 4:2

Grace . . . . Romans 5:7,8; 1 Corinthians 15:10; 2 Corinthians 9:8; 12:9; 2 Peter 3:18; Ephesians 2:8,9; Titus 3:7; 1 Peter 4:7-10; 5:5,10; Romans 3:24,25; Hebrews 12:28; Titus 2:11-14

Discouragement Isaiah 40:28-31; Romans 5:8; John 3:16; Romans 8:28,31-39; 15:4,13; Matthew 28:20; 17:19-21; 19:26; John 14:1-3; Galatians 6:9; 2 Thessalonians 2:16; Hebrews 11:1; 1 Peter 1:21; Psalms 38:15; 2 Corinthians 3:5

Complaining . . . Psalm 142:1,2; Philippians 2:14-16; 1 Corinthians 10:9-13; James 5:8,9; 1 Thessalonians 5:18; Colossians 3:17; 4:6; Hebrews 12:14,15

Contentment. . . Philippians 4:11-13,19; 1 Timothy 6:6-8; Hebrews 13:5; Proverbs 30:7-9; Psalm 37:3-7

Peace . . . . Proverbs 15:16,17; 1 Peter 5:14; Isaiah 26:3; Matthew 5:9; Luke 2:14; John 14:27; Philippians 4:4-7; Colossians 3:15; 2 Thessalonians 3:16; John 16:33; Romans 5:1; 8:6; 14:17; 15:13,33; Galatians 5:22,23

Trial . . . . Isaiah 26:3; 1 Peter 4:12-14; 1 Corinthians 10:13; Deuteronomy 13:3; Romans 8:35-39; Hebrews 2:18; 4:15,16; 12:3,4; James 1:2-4, 12-15; 4:7; 1 Peter 1:6,7; 2 Peter 2:9; 1 John 4:4; 1 Peter 5:9,10; 2 Timothy 2:3

Submission . . . . Mark 14:32-36; James 4:6-10; Hebrews 5:7,8; 1 Timothy 2:11-13; 1 Peter 3:1-6; 5:6,7; Ephesians 5:21-33; Luke 2:51 (think of "submit" as "give yourself")

Joy . . . . Psalm 30:5; 16:11; 1 Peter 1:6-9; John 15:11; 16:24; Romans 14:17; Nehemiah 8:9,10; Galatians 5:22,23; Philippians 4:4; Romans 5:2,11; 12:12; 15:13; 1 Thessalonians 5:16; Jude 24,25; Revelation 21:1-4

Speech . . . . Proverbs 15:1; 16:24; 17:28; 21:23; 25:11; 31:26; Matthew 12:37; Luke 6:45; Ephesians

4:22,25,29; Philippians 1:27; Colossians 4:6;
James 1:19,21,26; 3:2; 1 Peter 3:10,11,15,16;
Revelation 14:1-5

Worry . . . . Psalm 37:1-6; Matthew 6:25-33; Philippians
4:4-7; Hebrews 13:5; Luke 8:14; Psalm 37:25;
139;23

Worship . . . . John 4:23,24; Luke 4:8; Romans 12:1-21; 1 Corinthians 6:19,20; 10:31; Psalm 29:1,2; Hebrews
10:25; 12:28; 1 Peter 2:5; Psalm 84:1-4,10;
95:6; 27:4;100; 122:1; Revelation 4,5; 7:9-17;
11:15-19; 14:1-7; 15:2-4; 19:1-10

Dishonesty . . . . . . Proverbs 3:27; Jeremiah 22:13; Hosea 4:12;
Luke 16:1-8; 1 Thessalonians 4:6; Jeremiah 17:9;
Psalm 5:6; 1 Peter 2:21-25; James 4:17; John
8:44; Revelation 22:15; Ephesians 4:28,29; Colossians 3:5-10; Matthew 12:33-37

Obedience . . . . . . 1 Samuel 15:22,23; Matthew 11:28-30; 1 John
5:3; 2 John 6; Romans 6:16; Hebrews 5:7-9;
Matthew 7:21-27; John 14:15,21,23,24; Ecclesiastes 12:13; Ephesians 6:6-8; Philippians
2:12-16; Hebrews 13:16; James 1:22-25

Resentment. . . . . . Ephesians 4:31,32; Colossians 3:5-17; Matthew
5:43-48; Mark 11:25; James 2:13; Hebrews
12:14,15; Ephesians 5:1,2; 1 Corinthians 13:4-6

Freedom . . . . John 8:32-36; Romans 5:15-21; Galatians 5:1;
3:25-28; Romans 8:1,2; 2 Corinthians 3:17

Salvation. . . . . Isaiah 1:18; Psalm 91:14-16; Luke 7:47; 19:10;
Acts 4:12; Romans 1:16,17; 5:1,2; 10:10; 1 Cor-
inthians 1:18; Philippians 2:12-16; Galatians 1:4;
Colossians 1:20-27; 1 Thessalonians 5:8,9; 2
Timothy 3:15; Titus 2:11; 3:3-7; Hebrews 7:25; 2
Peter 3:9,15; 1 John 2:25; Jude 3

Forgiveness. . . . . . Matthew 6:12; Mark 11:25,26; Luke 6:35-37;
17:1-4; Romans 12:14-19; 1 Corinthians 4:12;
Ephesians 4:32; Colossians 3:13; 1 Peter 3:9; 1
John 1:9; Luke 23:34

Fear . . . . Psalm 4:8; 23; 27:1-3; Luke 12:4,5; Hebrews
13:6; 2 Timothy 1:7; 1 Jhn 4:18; Psalm 46:1-3;
Luke 12:32

A *Study of Prayer*

Pride . . . . Proverbs 6:16,17; 8:13; 11:2,12; 13:10; 16:5,18,19; 18:12; 21:4; 27:2; 29:23; Mark 7:20-22; 1 John 2:15-17

Family . . . . Ephesiains 5:21-6:4; Romans 8:14-17; Matthew 10:34-39; 1 Corinthians 11:3; Colossians 3:18-21; Titus 2:1-8; 1 Peter 3:1-7; Proverbs 31:10-31; 12:4; 14:1; 18:22; 19:13,14; 25:24; Matthew 12:50; John 14:1-3; 1 John 3:1

Courage . . . . 2 Timothy 1:7; 1 Corinthians 16:13; Joshua 24:14,15; 2 Chronicles 32:7,8; Hebrews 13:6; Luke 12:32; Psalm 23; 20:7; 46:1-3; Isaiah 41:13; Psalm 9:10; 2 Kings 6:14-17

Jealousy . . . . Proverbs 6:34; Job 5:2; Proverbs 14:30; 23:17 27:4; Song of Solomon 8:6; Romans 1:28-31; 13:13-14; 1 Corinthians 13:4; Galatians 5:19-21,26; Titus 3:3-7; James 3:14; 1 Peter 2:1-5, Matthew 27:17,18

Wisdom . . . . James 1:5-8; Psalm 111:10; Proverbs 12:1,8,15; 13:15,16; 15:33; 16:16; 11:22; 21:30,31; 31:26; John 8:31,32; Matthew 7:7,8,24-27; 1 Corinthians 13:11; 14:20; 2 Corinthians 2:11; 8:7; Ephesians 5:15-17; 2 Timothy 3:15; James 3:13; Colossians 2:8

Patience . . . . Psalm 37:7-9; Proverbs 15:18; Ecclesiastes 7:8,9; Lamentations 3:26,27; Luke 8:15; 21:19; Romans 2:7; 5:1-5; 12:12; 15:4,5; 1 Corinthians 13:4-6; Galatians 6:9; Ephesians 4:1,2; Colossians 1:10,11; 3:12,13; 1 Thessalonians 1:3; 5:14; 2 Thessalonians 3:5; 1 Timothy 6:11; 2 Timothy 2:22-26; Hebrews 12:1,2; James 1,3,4; 5:7,8; 1 Peter 2:19-25; 2 Peter 1:5-11; Revelation 14:12

Anger . . . . Psalm 37:8; Proverbs 12:16; 14:17,26; 15:1,18; 16:32; 19:11,19; 22:24,25; 25:28; 27:3,4; 29:8,9,22; 30:33; Ecclesiastes 7:9; Jonah 4:4; Matthew 5:21-26; Galatians 5:19-21; Ephesians 4:26-31; Colossians 3:5-10

33

Self-Control . . . . . 2 Peter 1:5-11; Luke 9:23,24; Proverbs 16:32;
Matthew 5:5; Ephesians 5:1,2; Matthew 5:48;
Luke 18:27-30; Mark 12:41-44; John 12:23-35;
Romans 13:14; 15:1-5; 1 Corinthians 6:12;
8:10-13; 9:25-27; Galatians 2:20; 5:16-24; Colossians 3:5-10; 2 Timothy 2:3-5; Titus 2:11-14;
1 Peter 2:11-15; 1 Peter 4:1,2; Matthew 6:16-18
1 Peter 4:1,2; Matthew 6:16-18

His Purpose . . . . . Psalm 139:13-17; Matthew 25:14-30,34-40;
for Me   Romans 12; Luke 9:23,24; Ephesians 4:15,16;
Titus 2:3,5; 1 Peter 2:9,21-25; Romans 7:4;
8:28; 1 Corinthians 10:31; Matthew 5:43-48;
John 14:1-3; Revelation 21:1-5; 22:1-5

Silent Hour
Meditation Questions

(Suggested time length: 25 minutes)

Have I accepted Jesus' standards as the standards for my life?

Am I self-righteous or am I able to yield when I'm in the wrong?

Do I erase worry by going to my Father's word, and by prayer?

Am I able to overcome difficulties alone most of the time, or must I always run to others?

Is each day a precious gift to me from my Father, to be filled with good for His sake with thanksgiving; or is it a cross to bear?

Does the thought of the brevity of life help me to use each hour well?

Have I lost my concern for self to find God in others?

".......that Christ may dwell in your hearts through faith;
to the end that ye, being rooted and grounded in love...."
Ephesians 3:17

Group Discussion or Thought Questions to Summarize Part II

Did I use my silent time to its fullest?

Write out, or share, any insight gained. If you prayed for another's problem, especially a person in the group, share any insights for them.

Was this application of the Scriptures an increased source of power in prayer?

Would you, or did you, add any references to the list for your word, or an additional word with references of your own?

Why do we fail to receive when we ask in prayer?

James 4:3 _____

Mark 11:24; James 1:6,7 _____

Mark 11:25 _____

Isaiah 59:1; John 15:7,8 _____

Luke 18:1-14 _____

Romans 8:26-28; Luke 22:39-44 _____

_____

John 11:3,43,44 _____

2 Corinthians 12:8,9 _____

PART III

My Prayer for Those
I Love Best

A wife and mother's prayer are crowded with loved ones' needs.

CHAPTER 5

Prayer and My Home Relationships

Prayer is lifting up those I love
  to Someone who loves them even
  more than I do.
    Prayer is the glue that holds marriages
    together, united in heart and happy.
      Prayer is the secret component of a blessed
      physical union in marriage.

What happens when we begin to pray seriously, with deepened dedication to developing a closeness to our Father? Oh, so many blessings come flooding into our lives that are unique to each individual and her situation and needs! Among all these blessings, some will be unique, ours alone for our situation sent by God through our dedication to a more meaningful prayer life, and discovered by each of those who are growing in this grace. Let us consider one of these shared blessings: God is given room to work through us to answer the needs of others. Who are the "others" in our lives for whom we most want to be everything that God can help us to be? Our families are the closest to our hearts, so as we enlarge our circle of prayer, we move from ourselves to include those in our home where our hearts are.

Jehovah God reveals Himself to us in terms of family relationship, as our Father, and Jesus as Son. His care is for individuals, often expressed in family associations. The Bible is abundant in records of family life, and guidance for family conduct and training.

Jesus and Family Relationships

Jesus, our mediator, understands what it means to be a human in a family. When the Father sent Jesus to live as we live, and feel what we feel, He set His Son in a family as the oldest of at least seven children (Matthew 13:55,56), the position He occupies for eternity as our elder Brother. Jesus knew about growing up in submission to parents (Luke 2:51). The maturing Youngster would observe a Daddy who worked hard and had to deal with all the types of customers our men must handle today — those who would not pay, those who were difficult to please, those whose demands placed the carpenter under pressure. He would see the wife and mother of a household struggle along with her husband to feed and clothe an expanding brood as one pregnancy followed another. The Nazareth home would have had childhood diseases, personality conflicts, daily chores, heartache and laughter. He would mourn the loss of Joseph and assume as the eldest son care for His widowed mother and the younger children for a time. Yes, Jesus knew family life because He had been a part of one in the same way we are.

Do you remember a busy day in the life of Jesus, as Mark 1:21 records it for us, when He taught in the synagogue at Capernaum and cast out an unclean spirit to free a man? After the morning of preaching and healing, doing what we would consider God's important missionary work, He goes home with Simon and Andrew. Away from the crowds, away from the narrowed eyes of those carefully measuring His words for faults, after a morning of self-giving, emotionally draining work, Jesus is astonishing for what He does not demand: quiet, time to rest, or food to refresh His energy. Jesus immediately responded to a need in that home by healing Simon's mother-in-law of a serious fever (as Dr. Luke describes the illness, 4:38). Oh, how we can treasure this incident: It tells us so much about our Savior:

> He cares about women,
> He responds to women's needs,
> He considers home important,
> He regards families worthy to
> receive His full attention and help

It seems He needed no great audience to impress. The family was important enough to draw His best from Him. He gave of His love to a family that had no influence with the Romans, or the rulers of the Jews and that had no substantial wealth to support His work.

The home of Mary, Martha and Lazarus was a blessing to Him of quiet loving friendship. We can't help but notice that His first miracle was performed at a village wedding to celebrate the beginning of a new family — an unnamed couple. Homes and family relationships are as much a part of Jesus' ministry as teaching the crowds.

Jesus Healed in the Family Circle

There are four of His healings that especially reveal His compassion for families and their relationships. A distraught father had brought his epileptic son to be healed. Jesus was away on the mount with Peter, James and John. The disciples had attempted to heal the boy and failed. Jesus cures the boy, lifting him up by the hand. When the disciples questioned Him concerning their failure, He answers, "This kind can come out by nothing, save prayer". Was He saying that they weren't living close enough to God (Mark 9:14-29)?

Then there was the day Jairus fell at Jesus feet begging Him to come to his house for his twelve-year-old daughter was critically ill. Jesus immediately begins to walk toward the troubled home, the disciples and a crowd following Him. It is truly a life and death situation to save a suffering child. We are startled to see Jesus stop and address the crowd, asking, "Who is it that touched me"? The panic rising in Jairus' heart must have reached desperation! The woman had been hemorrhaging for as many years as Jairus' little girl had lived! She had spent all she had on physicians but her condition had not improved. Under the Mosaic law, she would have been unable to attend worship or to be close to her family (Leviticus 15:19-30). Her suffering was not only physical but one of loneliness for she had been denied personal affectionate relationships for *twelve years*. Jesus does not rebuke her for interrupting Him at such a time. Instead He lovingly says, "Daughter, thy faith hath made thee whole". *Daughter!* Jesus blesses her with a fond family title. It is at that moment one comes from Jairus' house with the tragic news of the girl's death. Jesus encourages Jairus to believe and resumes His walk toward the child. We know the end of the event was triumph over death (Luke 8:41-56). And Jesus tells us God cares like that!

The most touching account of a healing in Jesus' ministry was the unasked raising from the dead of the only son of the widow of Nain. There was no request, no plea. Perhaps in her grief, the widow was unaware of the group coming toward the procession where her heart was dead, being carried to a grave. Jesus was deeply moved by the poignancy, the tragedy, and the widow's anguish. Tenderly, the Lord of Life restores the only son, "and he gave him to his mother" (Luke 7:11-15). "Jesus Christ is the same yesterday and today, yea and forever" (Hebrews 13:8). He cares about homes and is deeply moved by the troubled hours in our relationships.

Jesus Understood Mothers, Loved Children

He seemed to have a special place in His heart for mothers. In the upper room, He used the example of a woman in childbirth to strengthen His disciples for the dark hours soon to overwhelm them, "A woman when she is in travail hath sorrow, because her hour is come: but when she is delivered of the child, she remembereth no more the anguish, for the joy that a man is born into the world" (John 16:21). That last agonizing walk to Golgatha, He spoke with tender understanding to women who were weeping for Him, "Daughters of Jerusalem, weep not for me, but weep for yourselves, and for your children. For behold, the days are coming, in which they shall say, Blessed are the barren, and the wombs that never bare, and the breasts that never gave suck" (Luke 23:28,29). And what of the day that the little ones were almost prevented from being with Him? His response was deep displeasure and a profound teaching, "Suffer the little children to come unto me; forbid them not: for to such belongeth the kingdom of God. Verily I say unto you, Whosoever shall not receive the kingdom of God as a little child, he shall in no wise enter in". Jesus clearly values childhood and loves little ones, and Mark adds this touching brushstroke to the picture, "And he took them in his arms, and blessed them, laying his hands upon them" (Mark 10:13-16). Surely the children had some among them who had dirty pants, or sticky faces.

Think about Jesus' teachings and how many of His examples had to do with family concerns: mending clothes, planting, preparing food, sharing with neighbors, widowhood, losing money, a father with two sons (in two different family situations).

The evidence is overwhelming proof that we can talk to God about anything — anything, Beloved, concerning our home relationships with the confident expectation that He will listen with a caring heart and reach out to us.

Destruction of the Home

The generation in which we live is marked by the breakup of homes. It seems the home that has not been tarnished by divorce or separation is becoming increasingly rare.

What is the greatest single factor contributing to the destruction of marriage? Is it sex, or money problems, or in-law problems, or infidelity, or selfishness? Many experts in family relations tell us it is none of these. Their information points out the greatest single factor in the breaking up of homes is a failure in communication. Two people drift apart who one day stood together with stars in their eyes and hope in their hearts, eagerly pledging before God to love each other until the end of their earthly life. It was not a planned withdrawal from each other. Perhaps there is no legal separation, but even under the same roof the two live separate lives, each in their own personal world, and each of them lonely.

Could prayer prevent this alienation? It seems that prayer can be a strong bond between the three involved in a marriage (God, husband and wife) opening communication between the three, and allowing God who created marriage to guide and enrich and bless the two imperfect humans struggling to stay together and make a good life. In the last year or so, three different religious groups have announced their discovery of the power in prayer to contribute to the quality and stability of marriages. The statistics they gave were roughly the same:

Where there was no religion in the home, one in four ended in divorce;

When couples attended worship assemblies together, one in fifty-four divorced;

When couples prayed together every day, only one in five-hundred terminated in divorce.

Are you startled by these statements? Divorce is in the church more often than we like to admit. Why are we surprised when we learn Jesus' teachings really work, and work with *power*? His great promise concerning the power of prayer is also effective in marriage, "Again I say to you, that if two of you shall agree on earth as touching anything that they shall ask, it shall be done for them of my Father who is in heaven. For where two or three are gathered together in my name, there am I in the midst of them" (Matthew 18:19,20). If the two in a marriage agree on wanting God's will done in their lives personally and in their combined relationship, and pray together, the blessing is theirs! Whether they

41

pray aloud or silently, if they pray together, holding hands, Jesus "in whom all things hang together" (Colossians 1:17) will hold the two lives together in Him who created marriage, and for Whom both live to glorify.

Does all this sound too simplistic to be a practical solution to a complex problem? What about the statistics? Wouldn't it be worth a trial? What would be the value to a couple to realize more and more the oneness for which God created marriage, the beauty and perfection and joy in the relationship of Jesus and His church (Ephesians 5:21-33). To bring this about, we must learn to unfold our hearts and minds fully before God, to pray about everything in our marriage relationship. Everything includes the needs, the hopes, the budget, the words you speak to each other and most of all the love for each other in all its expressions. The release of our inner selves to God welcomes Him into the relationship, and the oneness you work toward will begin to grow in your life together — the oneness He planned when He created marriage.

God and Our Intimate Times in Marriage

One of the most sacred blessings the Father gave marriage is the physical union. Our generation has twisted the pleasure of sex away from the commitment of two people to each other for life, and made it an end in itself. Without love, with the pledge of two hearts, sexual pleasure fails to satisfy the emotional and spiritual needs, leaving behind guilt feelings, loneliness, and the sense of something missing. And something is missing — the blessings God intended. For those who love each other, the physical union is good from the wedding night, but for those who pray together, each year the sexual togetherness deepens and heightens with blessing. Prayer in a marriage lets God move in this most intimate relationship to free us from selfishness, to increase our senstitivity to each other, to enrich the satisfaction, the joy, the fulfillment of our coming together as He planned. The physical union is a gift from a Father who cares whether or not we have good health, spiritual life, and a happy life together with our husbands. Life becomes wholesome and balanced when the Creator is trusted to guide His created beings, and prayer is the channel that keeps us in touch with His wisdom.

For the Seeker

1. On a scale of 1-10, how do you think God would rate the success of your marriage relationship? _____
List the Scripture references on which you based your rating.
_____
_____

2. Does the author's description of Jesus' Nazareth home life and ministry enable you to think of Him as more personally in touch with your marriage relationship? Read Hebrews 2:17 and 4:15,16. Is there an area of your marital relationship that isn't all you deeply yearn for it to be? Have you prayed about your needs? Did you listen for an answer? _____
_____

3. Mother Teresa, the Nobel Prize-winning, Yugoslav-born nun-missionary said, "Loneliness and the feeling of being unwanted is the most terrible poverty". Loneliness creeps into marriage relationships too, even Christian marriage. Wouldn't it be worth trying to re-establish the communication by claiming the promise of Matthew 18:19,20? The Mediator who loves each of you can answer the silent cries of both hearts when·they are open to Him. Five minutes a day to hold hands and pray together can be found even in the busiest of schedules, can't it?

4. What does prayer have to do with the marriage relationship?
Read and apply:
Colossians 3:17 _____
Philippians 4:4-7 _____
1 Peter 3:7 _____
1 Corinthians 7:5 _____

5. Meditate on these Scriptures:
1 Corinthians 7:4 _____
Ephesians 4:31,32 _____
Ephesians 5:21,22-24 _____
Colossians 3:18 _____
As a wife, am I as responsive to my husband and as sensitive to his needs as I was when we were newly-weds? What changes do these Scriptures show me that I must make in myself to follow God's plan for marriage? _____
_____
_____

What did I find that I am already doing that God planned for my role as a wife? _____

_____

6. Are my prayers concerning my marriage partner more likely to be for changing him to conform to my desires, or for changing me to be the partner God wants me to be? Do I ask God to show me how to grow into the helpmeet suitable for my husband, bringing into being a happier home, or do I expect God to work a miracle in my husband?

Ephesians 5:1,2 has a powerful teaching: we are to imitate God's own behavior.

Ephesians 5:22 speaks to wives teaching us that we are to treat our husbands like we would treat Jesus.

Perhaps if wives concentrated on the roles God planned for them in marriage, and let Him take care of our husband's attitudes and outlook, He could guide and mold happier homes?

List one step you can make toward the goal God gave us in:
Ephesians 5:1,2 _____
Ephesians 5:22 _____

7. Thought question:

Good husbands work hard *for* their wives and sometimes have little time to spend *with* them. The relationship suffers because wives yearn for time shared with husbands.

God loves us. We are busy devoting our lives to His service, working *for* Him. Because we are so busy, has the time spent with Him diminished proportionately? Could it be our relationship with God has suffered? Spending time *for* Someone and spending time *with* Someone is not the same, is it?

8. Suggested memory work:
Philippians 4:4-7
Colossians 1:15-17 (This is a great passage to know on days when you feel you are flying apart).
Ephesians 3:19-24
Colossians 3:18,19
Ephesians 5:1,2

CHAPTER 6

Prayer, the Strength of Parenting

Prayer is the source of the strength, wisdom and laughter of parenting.
Prayer is the celebration of joy in a child between earthly parent and
heavenly Parent.

Prayer is hearing the answers to urgent parental pleas for
wisdom wrung from anguished, aching hearts.

The circle of family widens and those who most often bring us to our
knees, our children, enter our prayer life. Sometimes, when we are
praying about them, we pray as though we have forgotten that He to
whom we pray loves them even more than we do, and that the answer
He gives will be from the grace, and love and wisdom of their Father
who gave them to us. "Lo, children are a heritage of Jehovah; And the
fruit of the womb is his reward" (Psalm 127:3). They are only loans to
us. They came pure and innocent, spiritually clean before Him. Thank
God for prayer! We need His strength, and wisdom, and support to accomplish such a noble task. How He must love us to entrust us with His
precious little ones!

Prayer in the Daily Life of a Family

Prayer in the family's daily life forms a pattern in children's minds of
knowing God's strong arms are there to support them (even when you
are not), a pattern that will grow into their own personal relationship
with the Father.

How can prayer be of any practical assistance in nurturing children in
spiritual living, in maturing in the graces of living happily with others
(especially brothers and sisters), and in learning to be guided by God?
Our limits are self-imposed, for the creative Christian has only to ask
and her Father, the Creator, will guide.

Prayer is invaluable in discipline. An offspring sent off to school
scrubbed and sweet, returns with one button missing off her new coat,

45

her hem out half way around her dress, and her sash hanging from one seam. And she brings an uncomplimentary note from her teacher. Before you react, it could be a good idea if you sent her to her room to talk to God about her day, and you go to your room to pray about the situation. Afterwards, you will be a much more poised, controlled mother when you confront the sad little face to sort out what must be done. Especially since you could hear her quavering voice from her room, "I don't know why I did it, I'm sorry. I'm really, really sorry".

Prayer is the best way to preface the parting before school too. A brief prayer entrusting them to God's care and asking His help for them so they can do their best, sends children away secure in their importance to God and with high ideals for the day.

Prayer can be very special on birthdays. How blessed is the child whose Dad is a Christian and hears, him, each birthday, offer a prayer for her! What a bulwark in temptation and foundation for self-esteem.

Prayer, a Source of Closeness to God for the Older Child

Suppose the cheerleader tryouts or the parts in the play are to be auditioned, or the places on the little league team are to be assigned? Tell them, "I'll be praying for you to do your best", and repeat Romans 8:28 *with* them. If they make the team, or win the part in the play, or are voted a cheerleader, make it a special prayer of thanksgiving in the family devotional.

What if they don't make it? We must beware of platitudes or pat answers at that moment. They are hurting. They don't want to feel better, and they may think that they never will. They need sympathy and comfort. They need someone who will share their ache. What we say need not be profound, as long as it is said with love. Slip an arm around them and let them know you are sorry they are disappointed, and you understand how much it hurts. Let them know that, while they struggle with this pain, you will be praying for them. We can't take it for granted that they will know all this if we don't tell them. Later, we can teach and assist them to learn from these experiences that hurt.

Jesus left us an example of the power of prayer to strengthen others. The night before the cross, He spoke to one who would be especially tested, "Simon, Simon, behold, Satan asked to have you, that he might sift you as wheat; but I made supplication for thee, that thy faith fail not; and do thou, when once thou hast turned again, establish thy brethren. And he said unto him, Lord, I am ready to go both to prison and to death. And he said, I tell thee, Peter, the cock shall not crow this day, until thou shalt thrice deny that thou knowest me" (Luke 22:31-34). Bless his heart, Peter passionately loved the Master and dreamed lofty goals for himself. He failed. Sometimes our children are like Peter, dreaming impossible dreams, and failing, and sometimes *we* are like that too. For as long as he lived surely Peter could remember the voice of Jesus saying, "I made supplication for thee;" and it brought him courage and strength. The memory of our prayers may be the only strength that will sustain our precious children in an hour of temptation. The knowledge of our prayers may be a source of strength for them to meet difficult challenges.

Moving from General to Specific

Let's be specific in our prayers for our family members.
Do I need to apologize to my son?
Do I need to stop nagging my thirteen-year-old?
Help me to give more attention to the good things the children do and to put more laughter into our home relationships.

Help me to remove the words "I told you so" from my vocabulary. Did God preach at the Prodigal, "Uh, Huh, I knew it would turn out this way. Here you are back again, and you've lost all the money. Well! Aren't you proud of yourself!"?

Perhaps we should pray about a self-righteous martyr complex? Is there any attitude less attractive? Have you ever said, "If anything is repaired around here, I must do it or it doesn't get done", or "After all I've done for you, how could you do this to me!"? Jesus gave us an example of humility, self-denial, service. He not once demanded His rights as the Son of God. He not once stooped below His Divine dignity and allowed Himself to be used. It is a worthy aim to learn to be like Him.

We Cannot Change Others

Let's allow prayer and our study of the word to shine the light of truth on the weeds in our family life and change us, and then our homes will change. We can't change people, only God can do that. We can accept the family members for what they are, as we want to be accepted. We can trust them and their judgment, as we want to be trusted. We can say, "I'm sorry. I made a mistake", as we want them to say to us. We can spend time with them really listening to what they want to say, as we want them to listen to us. We can tell them, "I love you. I'm proud of you", as we want them to love and be proud of us. But, *we cannot change them*. We can learn to accept them, to live gracefully with them, to love and enjoy them through Jesus in prayer with thanksgiving.

Thanksgiving in Everything

Brother Paul gave us a terrific memory verse, "In everything give thanks; for this is the will of God in Christ Jesus to youward" (1 Thessalonians 5:18). Everything? Even when he doesn't make the team, or she loses the tryout? Maybe we find it difficult at that moment, but later thankfulness will apply for every prayer is answered from the loving wisdom of God, a Father.

"But", a mother says, "I have a situation I can't be thankful about. One of our grown children is not living close to God and has closed himself away from us. Our teen is in rebellion against our values. My heart is *crushed!* How can I be a Pollyanna and be thankful in all this heartache"?

God didn't promise us the easy way. Rather He told us of a cross to bear, self-denial, and family members who would not understand, turning against us. We can find reasons for thanksgiving in every circumstance, or He would not have commanded it. Beloved, you can grow to see Him through your fears. And when you do, you will find blessings to thank Him for. The mother's anguish kept her from thinking of God, her heart and thoughts were downcast wrapped around two antagonistic children. When she revealed her heart to her sisters in Christ, here are some of the comforting suggestions they gave her:

"You can be thankful for *time* — time from God to turn their lives around."

"You can be thankful for His patience with them and for loving them more than you do."

"You can be thankful for His gift of the ability to keep on loving even when the child seems not to return the love."

"You can be thankful that if the day should come that you must let the child go as the prodigal's Dad did, God will understand and strengthen you in that hour."

"You can be thankful you have only two who are breaking your heart; He has billions who hurt Him."

God Crowns Motherhood with Joy

There are heartaches in motherhood, pain we couldn't have imagined the day we first held that precious infant close in our arms. But there are joys along the way also beyond the imaginings of the mother of a firstborn infant. The joys are a gift of God, "He makes the barren woman to keep house, and to be a joyful mother of children" (Psalm 113:9). If we are not able to find our joy, or notice our laughter is not brightening our home as it once did, could it be we need to be closer to God in prayer? The love, the joy and the pain, each are gifts from our heavenly Father, to shape us for living forever with Him, and to grow in understanding His Father-heart's love for us.

The next workshop time, with reverent joy and thanksgiving, we will center our hearts in prayer around our home relationships. May God bless our time with Him, open our eyes to ways we can heal hurts and reach out more in love to build the home relationships He wants to give us.

For the Seeker

1. Think about giving your child away to someone else to bring up. Would you send along a detailed list of instructions?
   Think about God the Father giving you a child. (Psalm 127:3) Did he send along a detailed list of instructions? Does this little thought exercise help you to better identify with God's vital, personal interest in the quality of your parenting?

2. Who are the parents in the references here who prayed about their children? Search to see if/when their prayer was answered.
   Genesis 17:18 _____
   Genesis 25:21 _____
   Genesis 25:22 _____
   Genesis 30:1 _____
   Genesis 32:9-12 _____
   Judges 13:8 _____
   1 Samuel 1:10,11 _____
   2 Samuel 12:16 _____
   1 Chronicles 29:19 _____
   Ezra 8:21 _____
   Job 1:5 _____
   Luke 1:8-13 _____

3. List some examples of parental reaching out to Jesus for help in desperate situations. Give the reason for their coming to Him, His response and the reference.
   _____
   _____
   _____

4. Read through the book of Proverbs and record Scripture that relates to parenting. _____
   _____
   _____

5. Using a concordance, count the number of times the phrase "and his mother was" is found in 1 and 2 Kings and 1 and 2 Chronicles. What does this say to you about God's evaluation of a mother's influence? _____

6. When does personhood begin for a child in the eyes of God?
Ecclesiastes 11:5 _____
Psalm 139:13,14 _____
Job 10:8-12 _____
Isaiah 49:1,2 _____
Jeremiah 1:4,5 _____
Zechariah 12:1 _____

7. When in the life of a child should parental prayer for the child begin? _____

8. What are some of Jesus' sayings concerning children? List your references. _____

9. Suggested memory work:
   Luke 2:51 (A good verse for children to think about for it tells us Jesus, the Son of God, lived obediently under Joseph and Mary's authority).
   Matthew 14:19,20 (This verse presents a good thought for children too: Jesus liked leftovers).
   Psalm 127
   Romans 8:28
   Psalm 113:9

Prayer Workshop Time III

Using the Workshop II word list and procedure:
1. List the name of each person in your household. Write an appropriate Scripture verse next to each name.

2. List each person's name and what you feel is his/her greatest spiritual need:

3. List each person's name and by it write what you can do to help fulfill those spiritual needs. Be specific.

4. List each person's name, and write the quality you most appreciate in him/her. Resolve to concentrate on each one with sincere praise.

Silent Meditation Questions

(Suggested time length: 35 minutes)

Does my lack of self-control and sharp tongue prevent my family from giving and receiving affection?

Do I do the best that I can and prayerfully trust God to make up for the perfection of Jesus' character that is lacking in me?

Do I have an understanding heart that makes me aware of the needs of others, as Jesus would have me to be?

Am I forgiving in my home relationships: husband, children, friends, in-laws, even enemies?

Am I a good listener? Can I hear the silent needs being expressed?

How often have I prayed with my husband?

How often do we pray together as a family?

Am I fun to live with?

Are my children first in my life, or is my husband first?

Do I prepare my children for worship?

Living With My Father

What remarks do the children hear in the car on the way to assembly?

Do my children know the elders, and preacher?

Do I care for my physical body well enough to be patient with my family?

Do I elevate my husband to my children in my conversation and attitude?

Is a coffee cup a more familiar sight in my hand than my Bible?

Do I communicate love or anger in my discipline?

Am I teaching my children courage and faith or fear by my reactions to life?

Do my children unconsciously use good manners as a reflection of my attitude toward them?

Are Jesus' words familiar enough to my children for them to use them appropriately?

Have I taught my children to live peaceably (most of the time) with one another, or do I consider quarreling inevitable?

Am I a happy person?

"...may be strong to apprehend with all the saints what is the breadth and length and height and depth, and to know the love of Christ which passeth knowledge, that ye may be filled unto all the fullness of God."
...Ephesians 3:18,19...

A Mother's Prayer

Since Thou hast dared to trust me with
This life's supremest good,
Let me be found trustworthy in
The guard of Motherhood.

Keep me in touch with Thy great love
So patient, sure and wise,
That I, in seeing earthly deeds,
May look with heaven's eyes.

Redeem the faults of thought and deed,
Each poor example set,
Uphold me for the sake of little
Minds that don't forget.

Teach me to balance love between
Too little and too much —
Yet to maintain in all of life
The outward-going touch.

Be Thou my courage, strength of heart,
My soul's upreaching Way,
That little feet which follow mine May not be led astray.

Betty W. Stoffel, *Moments of Eternity*
Richmond: John Knox Press, 154, p.9)

The Kitchen Prayer

Lord of all pots and pans and things, since I've not time to be
A saint by doing lovely things or watching late with thee,
Or dreaming in the dawn of light or storming heaven's gates,
Make me a saint by getting meals and washing up the plates.
Although I must have Martha's hands, I have Mary's mind.
And when I black the boots and shoes, Thy sandals, Lord, I find.
I think of how they tread the earth, what time I scrub the floor.
Accept this meditation, Lord, I haven't time for more.
Warm all the kitchen with thy love, and light it with Thy peace.
Forgive me all my worrying and make my grumbling cease.
Thou who didst love to give man food, in room or by the sea,
Accept this service that I do, I do it unto Thee.

By Fay Inchfawn

Group Discussion or Thought Questions to Summarize Part III

How do you feel about applying the power of the Word to your family relationships? Give an example.

Did you gain any insights in the prayer time?

Did you discover a need to search out additional verses for someone? Or did you find that the spiritual need you had listed for someone in the household changed to another need you had not considered before you prayed?

Do you give praise naturally? Should you perhaps think about sharing more sincere appreciation for the good qualities in your family members with them?

Did you learn something about yourself in reflecting on the meditation questions? The Father blesses us serendipitously as we follow Jesus' example of caring in prayer for others.

PART IV

God's Family and My Heart

My prayers for the Lord's church are as one of a family of praying believers, born of His Word, walking in the light of His care, supported by His love.

CHAPTER 7

Prayer and My Relationship in the Church Family

Prayer is asking God to help me to do His will.
Prayer is my channel to God's wise guidance in living and serving as
He leads.
Prayer is a ministry of the concerned heart of faith.
Our discussion of prayer and the structured personal growth periods
have been planned toward the goal of strengthening our prayer lives in
the different relationships in which we move. We began with ourselves
and then included our families. Now we want to consider our relationships in the church, the dearest blessing we have outside our families.
These five discussions are, at best, brief explorations into complex
subjects. We can only touch the hem of the garment. However, it is
hoped the study can take us from wherever we are in a prayer relationship with God and point us toward growing even closer to Him.

We Are Family

Christians are a family in Jesus. No matter where we are in this world,
if there is a group of Christians meeting to worship, we can assemble
with them and feel we are not strangers but sisters in the Lord. We go
home with them for lunch and leave our purse on the bed and walk
away from it. That purse contains our identification, our passport, our
money, our necessities for travel. We are in a stranger's home, a
stranger we have met only hours before. The world would look upon
such trust as naive, even foolish! What the world cannot understand is
that we are *family*.

"But now in Christ Jesus ye that once were afar off are made nigh in the blood of Christ. For he is our peace, who made both one, and brake down the middle wall of partition, having abolished in his flesh the enmity, even the law of commandments contained in ordinances; that he might create in himself of the two one new man, so making peace and might reconcile them both in one body unto God through the cross, having slain the enmity thereby: and he came and preached peace to you that were afar off, and peace to them that were nigh: for through him we both have our access in one Spirit unto the Father. So then ye are no more strangers and sojourners, but ye are fellow-citizens with the saints, and of the household of God, being built upon the foundation of the apostles and prophets, Christ Jesus himself being the chief cornerstone; in whom each several building, fitly framed together, groweth into a holy temple in the Lord; in whom ye also are builded together for a habitation of God in the Spirit" (Ephesians 2:13-22).

What a glorious truth: the church is God's household! In other words, these verses in Ephesians tell us the glad good news that through Jesus, when we are members of His body, we are at home with God Himself! It is in His church that all barriers fall. Rich or poor, American or alien, Texan or Pennsylvanian, college graduate or high school dropout, middle-aged or teen, Republican or Democrat, homemaker or legal secretary, we can find acceptance, warmth, dignity, caring and usefulness in God's household, the church.

Relationships in God's Household

At least this is the plan Jesus died to bring to life. He knew that human beings needed to belong somewhere, to be a part of a noble cause to which they could dedicate themselves, and to have encouragement from the association with others who were also dedicated. He knew we needed these things almost as much as we needed cleansing from sin and the hope of eternal life. Why then do we find problems among the church family? The first century church had its difficulties. To read the epistles is to become impressed by the young churches' severe persecution, their knotty problems in personal relationships, as well as their theological misunderstandings. Paul even mentions two women, Euodia and Syntyche, in the Philippian church who had worked with him but who hadn't learned to have the mind of Christ and agree as one in Him (Philippians 4:2,3). Could humility have been the flaw in their attitudes? In the same letter, chapter 2:1-8, we read the word protrait of Jesus' humility and find the words, "Have this mind in you, which was also in Christ Jesus" (Philippians 2:5). It seems Euodia and Syntyche were genuinely committed to working for the Lord, but their dispositions and personalities had begun to irritate each other. Two women were marring the testimony of the church, the image of Jesus in the world. Rather than criticise them sharply, Paul begs them to follow the Master's example and asks a gentleman in the group to encourage them to reconcile.

The passage quoted from Ephesians 2 perhaps explains a part of the reason for difficulties within the household of faith. It says that we are "being built", and that we are "growing into a holy temple". Learning, growing, maturing and adjusting are painful processes. We know how personalities can conflict by observing our marriage relationship or our children as they are growing up together. We continue to love and accept one another in the home even when we don't agree no matter how emotional the disagreement may be. In fact, sons who dispute whether white is white and black is black with each other at home to the despair of their mother, on the football field or little league diamond will be each other's most enthusiastic fan! Loyalty in God's household must be as warm and as loyal as our love in our natural families. To achieve this goal of oneness and peace among sisters and brothers in the Lord demands humility, study of His word, yielding to the Spirit's guidance, and much prayer.

Acts, a Book of Prayer Fellowships

The first followers of Jesus, converted by the men trained by Him, were involved in prayerful fellowships. Before Pentecost, the apostles, the women, Mary the mother of Jesus and His earthly brothers were in Jerusalem together and "with one accord, continued stedfastly in prayer" (Acts 1:13,14). When they were to choose a man to replace Judas Iscariot, "they prayed" (Acts 1:24). After Pentecost, the infant church family "continued stedfastly with one accord in the temple", with worship and prayers (Acts 2:46). Peter and John are recorded as going to the temple at the hour of prayer (Acts 3:1). After Peter and John were arrested and threatened by the Sanhedrin, and released, they went immediately to the company of believers to report what had happened. The reaction of the church family is a beautiful outpouring of praise and prayer without one plea for deliverance from the clouds of persecution that were forming dark shadows of foreboding (Acts 4:24-31). We have only sampled four chapters of Acts to learn of the prayer life of the young church. Wouldn't you like to continue the study through the remainder of the Book? Prayer was the life-breath, the vitality, the strength of the early church.

It is to the church Jesus entrusted His gospel to share with the world. It is our task from His divine decree to call people home to God, welcoming them into the church family, the dwelling place on earth of the living God! The accomplishment of God's will and purpose in the church demands that the Lord's family be a praying fellowship, constantly in communication with Him.

Jesus Prayed for Us

The most complete prayer of Jesus recorded by the gospel writers is chapter seventeen of John. Some have titled this chapter, "Jesus' high priestly prayer." The shadow of the cross falls across Him when He speaks to His Father of the concerns closest to His heart. Let's notice verses twenty through twenty-three, "Neither for these only do I pray, but for them also that believe on me through their word; that they may all be one; even as thou, Father, art in me, and I in thee; that they may also be in us: that the world may believe that thou didst send me. And the glory which thou hast given me I have given unto them; that they may be one, even as we are one; I in them, and thou in me, that they may be perfected into one; that the world may know that thou didst send me, and lovedst them, even as thou lovedst me" (John 17:20-23). We are humbled by Jesus' prayer. His death agony was only a few hours away, and He, the Son of God, prayed for us! Now we know how Peter felt when he remembered Jesus' prayer for him (Luke 22:31-34). What did He pray for us? His prayer was for the church, for us, to be one in relationship as He and His Father are a unity of personal relationship. The importance of our unity is to lead the world to believe and know that God loves His own. Our love, our unlimited goodwill for one another, our ability to achieve unity in a world of disorder, unrest, and chaos will be the light, Jesus says, that shines from the window into a dark night of sin and despair calling people home to God, Calling the world home to grace, and peace, and hope, and love, and belonging, and salvation!

In the upper room the apostles had been graphically taught the lesson of humble service. After the Master had washed those twenty-four dirty feet, He taught the uncomfortable listening hearts, saying, "A new commandment I give unto you, that ye love one another; even as I have loved you, that ye also love one another. By this shall all men know that ye are my disciples, if ye have love one to another" (John 13:34,35). Beloved, we cannot learn Jesus' lesson without prayer, can we?

Do we love one another as Jesus loves us? No, we don't. We disagree. We forget to put others first. We fail to be understanding. We are unkind sometimes, without realizing it, lacking sensitivity to each other's feelings. Jesus is doing His part to bring our unity to perfection. He wipes out all differences, destroying every barrier, but we fumble and make a mess of our part. In our fourth workshop time, we will prayerfully consider our personal place in the church, and whether or not we can say to God, "Thy will be done on earth (through me) as it is in heaven" (Matthew 6:10).

Prayer and Our Attitudes

The relationships we share in God's family are important to Him. The New Testament has more teaching on the attitudes of the family members than on any other subject. We must learn to love each other, to encourage each other, to accept each other, to live gracefully with one another, for we hope to spend eternity together. There is no room in the church for pettiness, jealousy, irritation, harsh criticism, selfishness, grudge-nurturing, or pride, for these attitudes can keep us from heaven (Galatians 5:19-21). We know ourselves, our personal weaknesses, our failures, our selfishness. How then can we who know our own struggles with human nature criticize a sister in her effort in following the Lord? We cannot be judgmental with each other, Beloved, for when we are, we take the Master's authority, "Who art thou that judgest the servant of another? to his own Lord he standeth or falleth" (Romans 14:4). We are each His servants, under His direction. We have enough to do just living up to what we understand in the New Testament teachings without burdening ourselves with setting the church right as we see it. Thank God for elders who shepherd under His direction! We are free to grow and serve without that responsibility! We were not called to be in the Lord's body to have our own way, but to do His will.

Questions for Thoughtful Consideration

Could the following thought questions suggest areas in our relationships in the Lord that we need to consider prayerfully?

Am I approaching the understanding of Jesus with my Christian family?

61

Is my heart mature enough in Jesus to be able to love my fellow Christians just as they are, and not as I expect them to be?

Do I love my brothers and sisters in the Lord with a forgiving spirit? When I have my feelings hurt, when I am disappointed, when I feel slighted or neglected, can my love forgive any failure in my Christian family as I need forgiveness from my Father's loving mercy?

The bitter, unforgiving heart places a barrier between us and God; it breaks our fellowship with God. The Father is forgiving and merciful; and when we are cold-hearted, we have destroyed our family trait shared with Him (Mark 11:26).

Relationships and Worship

Let me interject an incident from the life of Robert Louis Stevenson. He held daily morning prayers with his family. Once during a prayer, he abruptly left the room. Later he returned explaining that he had suddenly remembered Jesus' words, "If therefore thou art offering thy gift at the altar, and there rememberest that thy brother hath aught against thee, leave there thy gift before the altar, and go thy way, first be reconciled to thy brother, and then come and offer thy gift" (Matthew 5:23,24). Mr. Stevenson recognized the insurmountable barrier to our prayer-life and to our worship, that broken relationships bring.

Jesus did not say, "If you have anything against your brother", but "If you know your brother has anything against you in his heart, you must make it right as a priority even before worship". Avoiding someone whom we feel disagrees with us or disapproves of us will not heal the wound in the body. Healing can only take place through loving concern for one another that is spoken and lived out in our attitudes. The New Testament teachings are powerful in us only when we study them with an open, receptive mind and apply them to ourselves. They only work when I understand it is my move first, "Do unto others as....." (Matthew 7:12). "Love one another, even as I have loved you", (John 15:12). "Be ye kind, tenderhearted, forgiving each other, even as God also in Christ forgave you" (Ephesians 4:32). The actions, the love, the kindness, the forgiveness is *my* responsibility, *my* duty.

Am I thoughtlessly selfish, forgetting that Jesus' love in me does not seek its own happiness but the happiness it can give others? Jesus lived a life of selfless love (Acts 10:38). He spent His important, pressure-filled days of ministry in doing kindnesses for those around Him. His desire was to serve, to do what He alone could do for others, and He did that service perfectly as God directed.

Do I love sacrificially? There was no demand from God that Jesus refused. If loving meant a cross, then He would bear it with loving grace. Do we have a limit in our yielding to God's will? Do we limit our goodwill for each other?

Prayer for Any Occasion

Never, O God, to be afraid to love,
Since out of love comes every lovely thing:
To find new courage fallen at my feet,
A flaming feather from an angel's wing:
To know the merciful, high-hearted dreams
Born to all men that cleanse and make them whole:
To take the gifts of life with fearless hands,
And when I give, to give with all my soul.

For the Seeker

1. Read through the letters to the seven churches in Revelation 2 and 3. Note the problems in the church family, or confronting the family, in each place, and the remedy given by the Spirit.

PLACE   PROBLEM   REMEDY

_____

_____

_____

_____

_____

_____

_____

What is the most dominant positive direction for you in your relationships in the family that you gained by studying the seven letters? _____

_____

2. Isn't it embarrassing that two women were the cause of damage to the church fellowship at Philippi? Describe the character and personality you imagine the courageous Christian brother had that was requested by Brother Paul to work with these sisters in their reconciliation. _____

_____

_____

Are there any men in your church family who have these
qualities?

_____

3. One of our perplexities in the church is that adults walk around in
    adult bodies, looking adult. In truth, some are babes in Christ, but
    with no sign, like diapers. We can mistake physical age for spiritual
    maturity. The expanded family of church members includes the
    whole spectrum of ages. In which spiritual age group do you see
    yourself? _____
    Why? _____

4. If you added the words "through me" in prayer as the author
    parenthetically did to Jesus' words excerpted from the pattern
    prayer, "Thy will be done on earth (through me) as it is in
    heaven", could I perhaps learn to see avenues of growth unex-
    plored before now? Is there a relationship I need to mend or
    strengthen? What is holding me back? _____

    _____

    _____

5. Do you agree that "we were not called to be in the Lord's body to
    have our own way but to do His will"? Do I seek His will for me,
    and accept with grace the opinions of others in matters of "how"
    to serve? _____

    Do I yield to the elders' guidance as Jesus' representatives of
    authority in the church and uphold their decisions to others
    (especially my children)? _____

6. Do I have limits beyond which I will not forgive? Ephesians 4:32

    _____

    _____

7. Suggested memory work:
    John 17:20-23
    John 13:34,35
    Mark 11:26
    Ephesians 2:19-22
    Philippians 2:5

CHAPTER 8

Prayer and My Ministry to His Glory

Prayer is yielding to the Father's directions of the use for my time and talents.

Prayer is discovering God's answers to troubled relationships.

Prayer for the church family is the delight of the Father's child.

Have I Found My Ministry in the Church?
I Have a Ministry?

What is a ministry? Perhaps a more comfortable word for our active, loving response to God's gift of salvation would be service. Service in the New Testament sense is both spiritual and practical. The church is a family, God's household (Ephesians 2:19-22). As our physical family members each have tasks that contribute to the practical meeting of needs in the home, and each has her own unique personal ways that lend loving support and joy to the family groups, in the same way each family member has practical and spiritual tasks in the church household.

We are the church wherever we are. In reality, everything we do is service for God. "Whether therefore ye eat, or drink or whatsoever ye do, do all to the glory of God" (1 Corinthians 10:31). This noble concept lends dignity to even the lowliest of duties, if in our hearts we work with love for God and the goal of presenting the completed task to Him.

65

We brush our teeth,
> change a diaper,
> telephone a friend,
> smile at a grocery clerk,
> brush a dog,
> drive a car,
> eat,
> teach a Bible class,
> visit the sick,
> encourage the elders,
> give money,
> garden,
> Whatever we do, we do it for His glory.

All of Life is Lived in a Temple

Every thing, every person in our lives is a loan from the Father to be cared for as His steward (1 Peter 4:10; Luke 12:35-37,41-44,48b). We read a tender reminder in James 1:16,17 of the source of all blessings, "the Father of lights", a title for God that refers to His creative activity. "Be not deceived, my beloved brethren. Every good gift and every perfect gift is from above, coming down from the Father of lights...." God is generously, creatively, pouring potential, opportunity and capability into our lives. Our task is to open our hearts and minds to know what He (the mind and head of the church-body) wishes us to do, to develop into, to cheerfully, obediently carry out in order for the church body to function healthily.

The Church-Body

If we were all pew-dusters, who would teach? If we were all classroom teachers, who would order the materials and pay the bills? If we all preached, who would visit the sick? If we all led singing, who would counsel the troubled? Brother Paul skillfully presents the church as a body in Romans 12:1-8 and Ephesians 4:11-16. We see clearly from these Scriptures that:
1. Each person is important to the body-life.
2. Each person has a vital function.
3. Each person serves in her own way as directed by Jesus for the accomplishment of a family goal impossible to achieve alone.

4. Each person considers the family members as of equal importance to herself before God, and herself as not inferior to any member.
5. Each person is devoted to loving and serving the same Lord.
6. Each person has the responsibility for finding and developing her personal ministry as part of the priesthood of believers.

Our Attitude in Service

It seems we are each born with a sign around our neck that reads, "I WANT TO BE IMPORTANT." As long as the Christian finds her importance in the loving joy of serving primarily from Jesus and her Father and their acceptance and guidance of her ministry, there is peace in her heart and the church family. But should she need notice from others and admiration from the family to perform at her best, there is the danger of resentment, anger, and jealousy creeping into her heart and putting an end to her ministry.

Jesus told a parable in Matthew 25:31-46 that outlines a six-point test for service. It demands no noble deeds that would heap honors upon us, no victories cheered by thousands of spectators, nothing that would keep our picture in the paper or bring us fame. Jesus speaks rather of kindness, of practical acts of caring done as though they were done for Him. He mentions no workshops to lead, no heavy schedule of speaking engagements, nor books to write.

We lose sight of Jesus' example in caring for God's own. And when we do, and He brings a work to our attention that is begging for someone to pitch in and set it in order, we may reject His bidding. Maybe the teachers' workroom needs straightening, or the fellowship hall cabinets are a mess, and we know it. If our attitude is not balanced and honest before the Lord, we could find ourselves upset because *someone* doesn't take care of these projects. Then if the Lord continues to nudge us, we might pray, "*Me?* Not *me,* Lord. Clean cabinets and workrooms? Surely not! I've far more important business to accomplish for You. Someone else with less talent and more time will do these chores."

Motives Are of Prime Importance

The *why* we select our ministry is important. It must be first, for Him, "Inasmuch as ye did it unto one of these my brethren, even the least, ye did it unto me." Our service must be motivated by love, unselfish, unconquerable benevolence (1 Corinthians 13:1-3). Our ministry must be the result of answered prayer with a firm conviction that the Lord wills our work to be done.

Beware of Self-Importance

There is a difficulty we meet in ourselves in the concept of prayer. Sometimes as we grow closer and closer to Jesus, and deeper and deeper into the study of His word, and more and more involved in serving Him, we unconsciously begin to judge ourselves as the only group of people God hears and answers. To illustrate:

There was an incident a few months ago involving two Christian ladies. Let's call them Mary and Dorcas. Mary had driven Dorcas to the mechanics to get her car where it had been left for repair. It was the middle of December, and the rush hour traffic was heavy. Dorcas was driving just in front of Mary as they returned home, when suddenly her car stopped with no warning. Mary managed to squeeze into a moving lane and drove away for help. The car then immediately behind Dorcas was hemmed in too. The man in the car came over to Dorcas and asked if there was anything he could to to help. He got in and tried to start her car. There was no response. The woman with him walked up about that time and asked if Dorcas would mind if they prayed about the problem. They bowed their heads and asked God to please help start the car because they were tying up traffic, and needed Him to take away the difficulty. After the prayer, the man reached over, turned the key again, and the car started. Dorcas offered to pay them, but they wouldn't accept any money. They told her that she should thank God for He deserved the credit. The couple was well-dressed, driving an expensive car.

Is this a strange coincidence? Did God answer their prayer? Were they Christians? What do you think? It really happened.

Do I Have a Task/Tasks Yet?

Have I found my ministry in the church family? Jesus demonstrated His love for His Father, and for us, by His obedience and His healing and teaching. Our ministry will not be one of raising loved ones from the dead or teaching with the authority of God's only begotten Son, and yet we have a ministry from God's divine decree. It is plain from a reading of Romans 12:1-8 that we each have a function vital to the life of the body. The example Brother Paul chooses of the fleshly body whose members neither argue nor envy each other, or quarrel about their relative importance, impresses us with the certainty that we have a task, a duty, a ministry to develop for Him and with His guidance. We are free to develop our own personal service ministry.

Our areas of ministry will change through the years, for we will grow and mature and become useful to Him in new ways. Because of this change and the privilege of being His, and being a part of His purposes on earth, our ministry must be a matter of prayer. It could be that there are new services we can give that we haven't thought about yet. It could be that we are spreading ourselves too thin by trying to do too many things, and it could be that God wants us to concentrate on fewer services and to perform them more effectively — and happily. Our love for God will not ring true to those who observe us, to those that we are trying to reach with salvation, if we are controlling our ministries and God is not. If we are phonies, we won't touch anyone's heart for Jesus. And we are phonies, when our prayer life is squeezed out of prime time in our lives — even by busy, busy service for Him.

I Can Pray Daily

There is always a way to set aside a daily prayer time. Someone says, "But, I have three preschoolers. I hardly have time to think, much less to pray." One young mother I know solved this problem by setting her alarm thirty minutes earlier to study and pray in quiet, uninterrupted meditation. She also shared a valuable insight with us. She realized that her children did not see her with her Bible except at family devotionals or worship assemblies. She wanted them to grow up knowing that the Scriptures are a daily, private joy for each Christian, so she would sit somewhere each day for a few minutes reading her Bible where the little ones could see her. She called no attention to her activity, and said that she rarely received any real strength from it because of the noisy play of the children nearby. She felt her example, the impression on young minds of commitment to God and the importance of His word was necessary to the foundation of faith in her children.

There is a little saying I embroidered on my curtains, in our family room, that helped me to keep my priorities in order many times when the ironing piled up, the phone rang off the wall, and the baby was cross all day: Praise, and Pray, and Peg away. If we can keep a thankful perspective in life, pray about our problems and then work steadily toward completing those tasks that keep the family going, God will add to our strength and grant us the wisdom to discern the important from the unimportant. Prayer brings strength, and answers, and victory!

Comfort the Young Mothers

Over and over I have heard young mothers, deeply disturbed, voice their concern about the limitations to their service. They feel guilty because they aren't serving in a more active outreach for Jesus. How sad that, somehow, the impression has been left with them that nurturing the young, being there to share their lives, to hear their prayers and tuck them in bed is not "Christian service" and ranks far below the missionary, teacher, elder and personal worker. Oh, how we need to pray for our own children! We are losing so many of them for God! Motherhood is a ministry of prime importance!

Ministries All Around Us

One powerful ministry in which we can all share in service is the ministry of prayer. Wouldn't it give you strength and courage to know that you were on someone's prayer list every day? Keeping a prayer list is a great ministry. It is a ministry that the teen, the shut-in, the elderly, the busy mother of a young family, can each participate in. There are so many who need our prayers! The list could include: the elders, the minister, the deacons, the missionaries, the teachers (especially the ones who teach us, or our children), the sick, the teens trying to grow up, the babes in Christ, the leaders of our nation, and the Russian leaders. The limit to a prayer list is set by personal interests and time.

Each Bible class teacher needs to keep her class roll as a prayer list. She may find herself spending a larger amount of time on the difficult student, and as a result finding answers to the problem of reaching that student for Jesus. The teacher who prays daily for her students sees the blessing of the class relationships becoming closer and warmer, and the truth more effectively taught and learned.

There is the quiet ministry of encouragement and supportive love we can fulfill simply by writing a note or sending a card to each one who responds to the invitation, or to the sick. A telephone ministry to absentees or shut-ins or the sick is a caring service for Jesus.

Prayer can open our eyes to the ministries around us that we have not seen. We have a place in the body, a function, a purpose. God made us to do His will. Prayer is our groping for the answer, for direction. It is His good pleasure to guide us.

You have noticed that the soaring, lyrical prayer of Brother Paul for the church that closes chapter three of the Ephesian letter has been given a few verses at a time concluding each Workshop Time sheet. To prepare our hearts for meditating and praying about our relationships and ministries in the church, let's begin our thoughts in the Amplified Bible with Brother Paul's inspired prayer for the church.

"For this reason (seeing the greatness of the plan by which you are built together in Christ), I bow my knees before the Lord Jesus Christ.

For whom every family in heaven and on earth is named — (that Father) from whom all fatherhood takes its title and derives its name.

May He grant you out of the rich treasury of His glory to be strengthened and reinforced with mighty power in the inner man by the (Holy) Spirit (Himself) — indwelling your inmost being and personality.

May Christ through your faith (actually) dwell — settle down, abide, make His permanent home — in your hearts! May you be rooted deep in love and founded securely on love,

70

That you may have the power and be strong to apprehend and grasp with all the saints (God's devoted people, the experience of that love) what is the breadth and length and height (of it);

(That you may really come) to know — practically, through experience for yourselves — the love of Christ, which far surpasses mere knowledge (without experience); that you may be filled (through all your being) unto all the fullness of God — (that is) may have the richest measure of the Divine Presence, and become a body wholly filled and flooded with God Himself!

Now to Him who, by (in consequence of) the (action of His) power that is at work within us, is able to (carry out His purpose and) do superabundantly, far over and above all that we (dare) ask or think — infinitely beyond our highest prayers, desires, thoughts, hopes or dreams —

To Him be the glory in the church and in Christ Jesus throughout all generations, for ever and ever, Amen — so be it" (Ephesians 3:14-21).

For the Seeker

1. Identify the ministries of the women in the following Scriptures:

	NAME/NAMES	MINISTRY
Luke 8:1-3		
Luke 10:38-42		
Luke 18:15-17		
Luke 21:1-4		
Mark 14:3-9		
Luke 23:49		
Luke 23:55		
Luke 24:1,2,10;Mark 16:7		
John 20:1-17		
Acts 1:13,14		
Acts 12:12		
Acts 12:13-15		
Acts 16:14,15,40		
Acts 18:1,2,26;Romans 16:3-5		
Romans 16:13		
1 Timothy 5:9,10		
2 Timothy 1:3-5		
Titus 2:3-5		
1 Peter 3:1,2		

2. Is my attitude prayerful as I seek to find my ministry or ministries? True prayer, a quieting of the mind and heart humbly before God, sincerely seeking His will, can change life attitudes and guard us from wrong motives in our work. The Devil subtly spoils our heart's relationship with the Father and His family by twisting our motives if we aren't careful.
List the motive for service in Matthew 25:40 _____

What are the six areas of service Jesus mentions in Matthew 25:34-36? Notice that these are practical services that the babes in Christ can share as well as the mature child of God. _____
_____
_____
_____

3. What is the service Jesus defines in Matthew 10:42? _____

Read what two or three commentaries have to say about this verse.

4. Jesus needed no acclaim from crowds to perform wonders. Who was present in the following Scriptures to see Him serve as only He could, and what wonder was done?
Mark 1:29-31 _____
Luke 8:22-25 _____
Luke 8:41,42,49-56 _____
John 4:1-30 _____
John 6:16-21 _____
Matthew 15:21-28 _____
Mark 7:32-37 _____
Luke 17:11-19 _____
Jesus blazed the way for His followers to live in an atmosphere of sensitivity to kindnesses that could bless, letting God walk in our bodies, moving through us in active love toward our fellowman. The summation of Jesus' ministry on earth in Acts 10:38 is our example.

5. Read the Scriptures below and research their principle in your resource books. Write out their meanings in your own words. Colossians 4:2 _____

1 Thessalonians 5:17,18 _____
_____

Does the study of these verses assist you to further define your goal of growth in prayer? In what way? _____
_____

6. Define "steward" in the New Testament sense as in 1 Peter 4:7-11.

_____

_____

7. Suggested memory verses:
     1 Corinthians 10:31
     Romans 12:3-8
     Ephesians 4:12-16
     Matthew 25:34-36,40
     1 Peter 4:7-11

Prayer

More things are wrought by prayer
Than this world dreams of. Wherefore, let thy
   voice
Rise like a fountain for me night and day.
For what are men better than sheep or goats
That nourish a blind life within the brain,
If, knowing God, they lift not hands of prayer
Both, for themselves and those who call them
   friend?
For so the whole round earth is every way
Bound by gold chains about the feet of God.

—Anonymous

Prayer Workshop Time IV

1. Let yourself soar without limits of any sort on your thoughts for God has no limits. My dreams for the church are

   Share with each other.
2. In ten years, I hope to be able to   _____

_____

_____ for God's glory in the church.
3. Read Ephesians 5:22,23 together and draw out the ideas that express the value of the church of Jesus.

4. Have I found my personal ministry for God? Share you concept of your ministry.

5. What are my talents, the services I can do best, and *enjoy* most? Romans 12:2-8 could hold some clues for my ministry in life. As I study the passage, I need to humbly consider the inestimable value of being a part of Jesus' blood-bought family, the called out.

Thought Questions for Meditation) (Suggested time length: 45 minutes)

Read the prayer of the church in Acts 4:24-31 and think of yourself in that group. Under such stress, what are your feelings? Are they the same feelings expressed in the prayer of that group?

Am I self-righteous or am I humbly able to yield when in the wrong?

Does my lack of self-control prevent God's family from giving and receiving affection and encouragement?

Have I found the humility to give up false pride that makes me try to lift myself up by pushing others down?

Do I have an understanding heart sensitive to others' needs as Jesus would have me to be?

Am I forgiving in my relationships? Ephesians 4:32; James 2:13

Am I able to wish a person only good even though I strongly differ with her?

Have I lost my concern for self to find God in others?

Am I fun to be with?

Am I ready and willing for God to use me as He sees fit and to win others for His sake?

What is my general attitude? Am I more of a critic, or complainer, or encourager? Do I practice Hebrews 10:24?

Do I have a problem with my attitude toward the church or one of my fellow Christians that I need to talk to God about so He can help me make my attitude right and take any necessary steps to heal the wound in the body?

List any Scriptures to study that relate to your problem. Write them out in full.

"Now unto Him who is able to do exceedingly abundantly above all tht we ask or think, according to the power that works in us, unto Him be the glory in the church and in Christ Jesus unto all generations forever and ever. Amen" (Ephesians 3:20,21).

Group Discussion or Thought Questions To Summarize Part IV

Did you have a new insight? Would you share it?

Were you convicted of a new ministry, or needed change in your service?

Did a meditation question speak to a particularly new thought for you?

Is prayer becoming less of a pious ritual to you and more of a communication vital to living? How will this attitude show itself in practical ways in your everyday walk with the Lord?

This little anonymous prayer could be applied to the motto "praise and pray and peg away",

> Thank God for dirty dishes,
>   They have a tale to tell,
> While others may go hungry
>   We're eating very well.
> With home, and health and happiness,
>   I shouldn't want to fuss,
> For by this stack of evidence,
>   God's very good to us.

Try to imagine your life without the family of God. Does the emptiness, the loneliness, the aimlessness of that sort of life help you value even more the supportive love and encouragement you have in Him?

PART V
Living With My Father

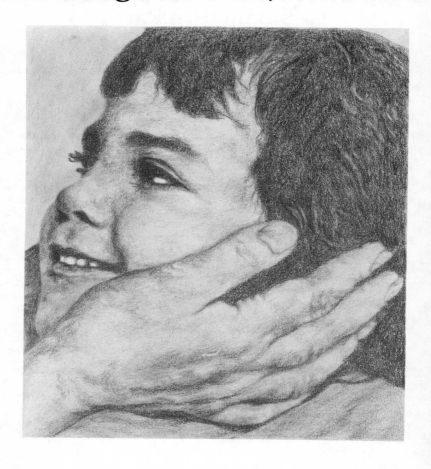

My relationship with Abba Father and myself is as affectionately warm as a little one with her Daddy.

CHAPTER 9

The Joy and the Agony

Prayer is bending our will to God's will for us.

Prayer is the communication between Father and daughter.

Prayer is losing the fear of rejection and baring our inner-most secret selves to Him for grace to meet our needs.

In reality prayer on its deepest level is not hoping to have our petitions answered, but rather a bending of our will to God's will for us. To have this quality of personal relationship with God demands time, dedication, work, study, a commitment to having a Father-daughter communication with Him.

We discovered that lack of communication is the number one reason that marriages fail. Similarly, lack of communication with God, failure to have a personal commitment to Bible study and prayer, is a prime reason why believers grow cold and drift away from God.

Jesus left us an example of how to live with God. Jesus knew the Scriptures. He loved His Father and constantly communicated in prayer with Him. One prayer He spoke is particularly graphic describing Jesus' attitude of prayer. He is standing in the dirt roadway, outside the tomb of his friend Lazarus. The stone has been rolled from the entrance by His command. "And Jesus lifted up His eyes, and said, Father, I thank thee that thou heardest me. And I knew that thou hearest me always; but because of the multitude tht standeth around I said it, that they may believe that thou didst send me" (John 11:41,42). He says that God heard Him and hears Him always. Don't these words express a constant silent communication with God? The spoken prayer was simply a continuation of a conversation between the Two who loved each other.

Jesus was completely open and honest with God, His Father. A relationship like this doesn't "just happen". It requires time, years of time, to build.

Breaking Down the Barriers

The agony in prayer is learning to be completely open with God, being able to uncover the corners of my will, and heart, and mind, and past, freely, trustingly allowing Him to look at me in the glare of His holiness. To do this, I must discipline myself to recognize the walls I have built to protect myself from the hurts people have given me that I have left standing between God and me. I must unlock that secret closet in my inmost self that I share with no one — not even God. I must learn to share my dreams, my hopes, my longings, my joys, my problems, my frustrations, even my moments of anger and inability to be forgiving.

To speak with God as to a loving Father, I must trust His love for me, expecting His mercy, and forgiveness, and grace, and acceptance with childlike faith. In the parable Jesus told in Luke 15 of the Father who was having problems with His two sons, the Father is God. What kind of heart, of parental attitude did the parable reveal about God Himself? Was the Father not telling us, "I'll love you no matter what you do, no matter where you go, no matter if you have wasted your days in a lifestyle I abhor. All I want is for you to come home to Me with an humble penitent heart". Jesus said that God is like this! We can be completely open with God because He loves us just the way we are, He accepts us through Jesus, and He will not reject us when we turn to Him for forgiveness, mercy, and grace.

People may reject us when we let them peek into our inner selves, but God won't. Revealing our secret sins to one who is most intimately acquainted with us can threaten earthly relationships, but not so with God. The Father meets our confessions with cleansing, healing and forgiveness. He lifts us from our knees to serve Him in joy. The free love of God is not ours because we have earned it or deserve it; His love was ours before we knew Him! "But God shows and clearly proves His own love for us by the fact that while we were still sinners, Christ, the Messiah, the Anointed One, died for us" (Romans 5:8 AMP). We know there is no need to pretend with God, but we avoid uncovering our hearts before Him even though we believe that He will receive us with dignity, and grace, and love. Our relationship with God will not be a warm, caring one until we can expose ourselves to the glare of His purity, goodness, and truth, and accept His grace to cover our hidden, secret sins, our weaknesses, our failures — all the things that cause us to have a small inner-self that is always lonely.

Oh to Never Be Lonely Again!

Loneliness is the affliction of each human. Small children feel loneliness and elderly people must deal with its pain as well. What was it God said before He created woman? "It is not good that the man should be alone...." (Genesis 2:18). Adam was truly alone, the only being of his kind on the earth. Somehow the loneliness problem was not solved by the addition of people. We can be as lonely in a stadium with sixty-thousand cheering fans as we are at home alone viewing the game on television. Suicides are the final desperate screams for someone to listen, to care. How many brides think as they walk the aisle toward their groom, "How happy I am! Ahead of me is companionship, someone who cares about me and understands me. Life will be peace and joy and love from this moment on!"? A bride finds soon enough that loneliness is still with her. We can never be as close to those we love here on earth as we feel the need to become. We hold a baby in our arms and love her so much we could just squeeze her until she becomes part of us again, but the separation remains. Even in our most personal moments with our husbands, there is a part of them we cannot share and a part of us they will never know.

Shut in with God

Loneliness! Why must we suffer the pain of loneliness? It was loneliness that turned the prodigal back to his Father. It was loneliness that tore the cry from Jesus' heart to God, "Eloi, Eloi, lama sabachthani? which is, being interpreted, My God my God, why hast thou forsaken me" (Mark 15:34)? There is our clue. Could it be that there is a part of us that will be lonely until we fill it with God's fellowship? Is loneliness one of the Father's ways to turn us to Him, to keep us needing Him, reaching out to Him until faith is lost in sight and we find the perfect loving relationship forever? So many times, women burden their marriage partners with expectations for a relationship that will be the source of all fulfillment and meaning in their lives. Or mothers, consciously or unconsciously, manipulate their children in their search for the answer to their loneliness. If only we could grasp the joyous fact that we are here to help each other to reach heaven, and God alone is the One we are seeking to be our dearest Companion. There are hours of shared love, pride in children, sorrow, fun in this life. We share one kind of relationship with husbands, another with children, still another with friends. Dear as these relationships are, no one is complete and can meet every need our heart longs to find. There is a part of us that the Father reserves for Himself alone. When we are feeling lonely, we are not shut away from everyone, misunderstood, friendless. When we are lonely, we are shut *in with* God.

David gave us an illustration in Psalm 142 of God's plan for our handling of loneliness. "Look upon my right hand, and see; For there is no man that knoweth me: Refuge hath failed me: No man careth for my soul" (v. 4). Daved voiced the anguished cry of the lonely heart. David's loneliness brought him to his knees, seeking God's closeness. The Psalm is a prayer for God's answer to isolation in distress, and ends with hope for a day when God has removed the affliction, a day when David can pray in thanksgiving and enjoy restored fellowship with others with a positive confirmation of faith, "...For thou wilt deal bountifully with me" (v. 7). Loneliness had shut David in with God and brought about a deeper faith in Him, a sense of dependance on His omniscience. Loneliness can do for us what it did for David, and for Jesus.

Jesus often withdrew from the crowds to be alone with His Father. The crowds gave Him attention, adoration, acclaim (granted, He certainly had His critics). Yet their closeness, the women who followed Him meeting His needs financially (Luke 8:1-3), the apostles He spoke to openly, none of these could give Him the loving companionship His Father gave.

Jesus Leads the Way

How do we go about developing the relationship with God that will approach the relationship Jesus shared with Him here on earth? How do we go about learning to share with God what is going on deep inside ourselves, all the things we share with no one else? We want to be God's women, and when we tell Him this, He replies, "The joy is on the other side of the cross. Meet Me there." The writer of Hebrews put it this way, "Therefore let us also, seeing we are compassed about with so great a cloud of witnesses, lay aside every weight, and the sin which doth so easily beset us, and let us run with patience the race that is set before us, looking unto Jesus the author and perfecter of our faith, who for the joy that was set before him endured the cross despising shame, and hath sat down at the right hand of the throne of God" (Hebrews 12:1,2). The answer is in the example of Jesus.

Let's look at Jesus in the agony of prayer as He prays in Gethsemane. He is alone; the only One on earth who can comprehend His total suffering. His disciples sleep — even those of the inner circle: Peter, James and John. His earthly brothers do not believe on Him (John 7:5). He is misunderstood, bitterly opposed and murderously hated by the religious leaders. Could the human part of Him long to return quietly to the haven of the Nazareth home, to love, to people who cared for Him? He was a master carpenter and could earn a living with His skill and live a secure, peaceful life. Surely Jesus knew the love of home in a way we never can. After all, He came so that we can someday share the perfect home with God, the Father, forever.

What was He facing in the Garden? He knew crucifixion. It was a common sight in Roman-occupied Judea. There would be torture, mockery, being whipped with leather thongs that would rip long ribbons of skin from His back exposing the raw meat underneath. There would be the sound of spikes driven through His body as He listened to the hammer blows, feeling the spikes driven through His body, feeling the spittle drying on His skin, and insects crawling on His open wounds — insects He could not brush off. He would know the hot flame of pain, searing His consciousness, flooding His being as His cross was lifted up and dropped into the hole prepared for it and then His body weight pulling down against the restraining nails. Blood would run into His eyes from the thorny crown clouding His vision — blood He was helpless to wipe away.

The Agony of Rejection

He faced the deep hurt of rejection by those to whom He had revealed His heart and to whom He had entrusted His message. He would be rejected by His friends, those who had received His healing, His love, His understanding. He would know rejection by all those He came in love to take home with Him. "No man careth for my soul." Such an agony of loneliness could only be borne by the Son of God.

Jesus would have struggled with the certainty of all these torments to come. But He recoiled before a pain more severe than the sum of them. On the cross, He would take upon Himself the sins of the world and for our sakes be separated from His Father for the only moments in eternity that He would ever know the loneliness of being outside their close relationship of love. "Him who knew no sin He made him to be sin on our behalf; that we might become the righteousness of God in Him" (2 Corinthians 5:21). He was totally alone, isolated from love on earth and from heaven as no other has ever been or ever will be. No wonder He sweat drops like blood as He prayed facing the cross!

When Doctor Luke describes the scene, he records "And being in agony..." (Luke 22:44). The Greek word he was guided to use for 'agony' is not a word for physical pain, but carries the meaning of one fighting a battle with sheer fear. Surely the responsibility of completing so great a task for God was heavy on his manly heart, while the association with evil it demanded was repugnant to His holy nature.

Prayer Life Like the Master's

What can we learn about prayer from Jesus in the Garden? Suppose we have a three-year-old who must have surgery to save his life, but which may leave him unable to walk. If we follow Jesus' example that He left us in Gethsemane, of prayer born of anguish, should our prayer for the child be, "Not my will but Thine be done"? Perhaps. Let's look and learn the deeper truth. "And he went forward a little, and fell on the ground and prayed that, if it were possible, the hour might pass away from him. And he said, "Abba, Father, all things are possible unto thee; remove this cup from me: howbeit not what I will, but what thou wilt" (Mark 14:35,36). Jesus in His intimate relationship with His Father: *first* told God how He would want things to be, *then* He prayed, "never the less, not my will, but Thine be done" (Luke 22:42). This is true communication with a Father who is loved and trusted with the faith of a child.

Jesus prays, "Abba, Father". Before Pentecost, which opened the way for mortals to become children of God, only Jesus could pray "Abba, Father". Abba is a word still used by children of the Syria/Palestine area. It was a word in Jesus' time on earth that corresponds to our "Daddy". It was the word for a Father when a little one climbed on His lap to say, "I hurted myself", or during family times of playing "horsey" on the floor. It could not be used by slaves. It was reserved for the children of the household in their private hours together. It was an affectionate term of endearment spoken in recognition of relationship.

Can you imagine the wrench to God's heart when He heard His Son, His beloved Son, who was a man thirty-three years old, on His face on the ground in agony, pleading, "Daddy! Please don't make Me do this if there is any other way!" As parents, we know the constricting pain of helplessness when we must stand by a suffering child. We cannot understand the depth of love for us that prevented God from forgetting us to save His only begotten Son. In thankful reverence we can only accept the fact and respond in love to His goodness and care for us. Jesus knew He was praying to a Father whose love could be trusted, whose will was only for good toward those who love Him.

The Meaning of Creation

From the pre-creation, God has longed for His beings to love Him, to choose to come home to Him forever. The heart of the Bible, the distilled essence of the reason for it all, is found in these words, "Precious in the sight of Jehovah is the death of his saints" (Psalm 116:15). The Father counts as *precious our safe homecoming to be with Him forever! His love is lonely for us until we are with Him, saved!* God, the Abba, Father, suffered the pangs of loneliness for His Son for us!

So if we follow Jesus' example in prayer for the precious toddler in surgery, our prayer would probably be something like this: "The little son You gave me is in Your hands, Father. Please be close to Him because I can't be there with him. Encircle him with your love as a watchful guard. Guide the hands working on his small body. Let him walk again. Let him be strong and straight, and live for You. Help me, Father, if Your will is not mine, to accept Your wisdom. Grant me the strength to bring up the boy to live a full life for Your glory." Jesus told God what He wanted, what He felt He needed, then spoke the acceptance of the Father's will over His own.

Victory and Joy

It is in communication with a Father that we find victory! Jesus' dying words were a shout of triumph, "And Jesus, crying with a loud voice, said, 'Father, into thy hands I commend My spirit:' and having said this He gave up the ghost" (Luke 23:46). After the agony, after we crucify our will, comes the joy! "Weeping may tarry for the night, but joy cometh in the morning" (Psalm 30:5). It will make all the difference in our dying hour, if we feel we are going out to meet a stranger, or an enemy, or whether we will simply fall asleep as Jesus did on the cross, in the strong supportive arms of a loving Abba, Father.

Perfection in Prayer

And we as Christians have the blessed, exalted privilege of using that intimate, precious, personal, private family word, Abba, for Jehovah God, as Jesus did (John 1:12; 1 John 3:1; Romans 8:15; Galatians 4:6). This is the ultimate intrinsic perfection of prayer, the agony and the joy in prayer, to be the open-hearted child with God, our heavenly Father, that we yearn for our own children to be with us.

Why should we work at being totally honest, totally open with God? The more open we are with Him, the more pliable we are in His hands, the more He can fill us with *His* light, *His* love, *His* kindness, *His* understanding, *His* mercy, *His* peace — *His* character. There is no need to grimly strain to achieve the relationship. Jesus helps us. He goes with us to our secret hiding places, our closets, our cluttered attics, and gently lowers our masks before the Father. He comes to live in our hearts, take our hand, and give us the courage to risk rejection by loving the ones around us as He did for our sake.

Vertizontal relationships find peace, "shalom", in Jesus through prayer, the great unifier. Jesus works in His mediation to be the magnetic force that holds all things together without the barriers of separation (Colossians 1:13-18). A renewed dedication to prayer will unify us with God, our Abba Father, through Jesus, our Savior. Prayer shared with our husbands will unify us with them, bringing out the beauty of our special relationship to each other, making the dual relationship a trinity as He planned in creation. Prayer will unify the church, giving Jesus room to move with power to guide, to love and strengthen, and to add to His family through vessels of clay.

When we cry, "Abba, Father", we will find Jehovah God more than a refuge in the crucible hours of sternest trial; we will know Him as Someone to love and to remember every day of our lives. We will see prayer at times as demanding no words, when our joy is simply to sit quietly and adore Him, thankful that He is with us and is our Abba.

Jesus is God who came to earth and moved in next door (John 1:14). He is God's dialogue, God's heart exposed, God involved in our human situation, telling us how very dear we are to Him — so precious that He could withhold His compassion from His Son to have us come to Him! Amazing grace! Amazing love! Surely we can reverently learn to reveal the deepest level of our inmost selves to Abba, Father. It is a lifetime struggle, a continuing discipline, with rewards of highest joys all along the way.

Beloved, we can go to God in prayer with the glad truth and security of 1 John 3:1 on our lips, "Behold what manner of love the Father hath bestowed upon us, that we should be called the children of God; and such we are".

May God bless the study of prayer we shared. May we all go home safely to be with our Abba, Father in serenity and joyous love forever through the sacrifice of our Savior, Jesus the Christ.

Father, Thank you for being our ABBA FATHER.

For the Seeker

1. Is there a true communication between God and me? Read John 15:7-10. Notice the word "abide". You remember the Greek meaning of "abide" is an enduring, inward, personal communion. Read the passage once more substituting the expanded Greek meaning for abide as you read. _____
   _____
   _____

2. Is God's love real to you? Do you read the parable of the Prodigal Father (Luke 15:11-24) and stand in awe rejoicing in the God of love receiving a filthy sinner......but with reservations that you could also be (lovingly) received by Him? Would the Father explain "Either you believe *all* my truths or *none* of them"? Write your thoughts about yourself as the son in the parable. _____
   _____
   _____
   _____

3. If God were to place price tags on His created universe, what price would He place on you?
   Romans 5:8 _____
   Luke 9:25 _____
   Matthew 10:29-31 _____
   Matthew 12:12 _____
   What value should I place on myself? _____
   _____

4. Can I begin to let lonely hours shut me in with God and take away the pain that Satan would have me suffer? Would this also take a

burden from my husband he senses as a pressure from me? What is the first step I plan to take to work creatively and positively toward handling loneliness shut in with God? _____

5. Do I pray as though I trust my Father with the truth of my feelings, or do I cover them with words I think He wants to hear as a teenager with a parent? Jesus said that the truth makes us free (John 8:32). How can truth, real, honest, bedrock truth free me in my personal prayer relationship with God? _____

Does 1 John 4:18,19 apply to a relationship of truth between my Abba Father and me? _____

6. Do I pray for escape from pain and difficult situations or for strength and faith and guidance to let them shape me into Jesus' image? Do I remember that beyond the cross is the joy? What difference does my relationship with God make in my attitude during times of pain or stress? Psalm 118:5 is the blessing of those who trusted Him and found victory. How would your "Psalm 118:5" paraphrase read? _____

7. We all love the precious privilege found in 1 John 3:1. Read what your resource books have to say about John 1:12 and our *right* to become God's child. _____

8. Read through Psalm 139:1-18,23,24 once more and exchange Abba Father for the names of God in these verses. What new thoughts did you have? What precious truths took on new meaning to thrill your heart? _____

9. Suggested memory verses:
   Psalm 116:15   Romans 8:15
   Romans 5:8   1 John 3:1
   Hebrews 12:1,2   Psalm 30:5
   2 Corinthians 5:21   Luke 22:42
   Mark 14:35,36   Psalm 139:1-18,23,24

Let me encourage you especially to determine to learn Psalm 139. It is a beautiful gift to give your Father. It will be a continuing blessing to give yourself.

CHAPTER 10

Prayer Workshop Time V

1. I want to share in communication with my Abba, Father in childlike faith. As a step toward such a simplified, basic revealing of myself, I want to share with Him:
The most interesting thing to me today has been _____
The most beautiful thing that I have seen today is _____
The kindest thing that someone has done for me today is _____
_____
The kindest thing I have done for someone today is _____
_____
(These four personal facts make a terrific basis for sharing our lives around the dinner table to make it a place of coming together in deeper understanding, patterning our association after Philippians 4:8. A good family rule is that these must be shared before criticism or complaint).

2. Read Psalms 130 and 51 aloud together.
Silently read the meditation thoughts and discuss together the thoughts to be personally completed.
I need to confess _____
Is there something I continue to push aside and avoid confessing to God? I need to acknowledge _____ as a weakness.
Do I have a weakness I refuse to admit to myself that I have? Example: I'm overweight and I blame it on metabolism, or I'm easily irritated and comfort myself with the excuse, "It's a family failing".
I need to find strength to _____
It might be a discipline of self, or enduring a problem with His grace, or learning to love someone I find unloveable.
I need to let go of _____
Examples: nagging, fear, resentment, any of the things that take time unnecessarily from my time of personal prayer and study, pride that keeps me seeking glory for myself from those around me, jealousy that invades my heart like a cancer and takes away my thankfulness from the undeserved blessings I have from God.

3. To me, prayer is _____
complete this sentence during your silent mediation time. Compare it with the same sentence you completed in your first workshop time. Have you matured in understanding, or enriched you concept of prayer?

86

Meditation Thoughts
(Suggested time length: 55: minutes)

Respond to these thoughts as you stand before the Father's throne stripped spiritually bare before Him.

Do I now totally and completely give myself to Abba, Father, and place myself under His management?

Am I the child to God that I wish my children would be to me?

Am I ready and willing for God to use me to win others?

Have I accepted Jesus' standards as the standards for my life?

How willing am I to sacrifice?

I need to confess _____ for it stands between God and me.

I need to acknowledge _____ as a weakness.

I need to accept forgiveness for _____ (1 John 1:7).

I need to find strength to _____

I need to let go of _____ to boost myself one step closer to being pliable clay in God's creative hands.

I deeply desire Abba, Father as the center of my heart, my thoughts, my will, my strength, and I will tell Him so now.

Group Discussion or Thought Questions
to Summarize Part V

Allow each person to respond to each topic.
1. Would you share any insight or new thought you have gained?
2. Is there anything you would like to say to any other person in the group?
3. Could you share an answer to the sentence completions in the thought questions that wouldn't be too personal?

4. Did you find a deeper understanding of prayer from our study?

"The grace of the Lord Jesus Christ,
   and the love of God,
     and the communion of the
      Holy Spirit,
       be with you all" (2 Corinthians 13:14).

"Sanctuary"

'Mid all the traffic of the ways, —
Turmoil without, within, —
Make in my heart a quiet place,
And come and dwell therein.

— A little shrine of quietness,
All sacred to Thyself,
Where Thou shalt all my soul possess,
And I may find myself;

— A little place of mystic grace
Of self and sin swept bare,
Where I may look upon Thy face,
And talk with Thee in prayer.

— John Oxenham
from *Selected Poems*

Benediction

The sun be warm and kind
To you,
The darkest night, some star
Shine through.
The dullest morn
A radiance brew.
And when dusk comes —
God's hand
To you.

FURTHER STUDY ON PRAYER

1. Read and mark each of the New Testament benedictions holding the thought that these words are for *Me*. For example: John 8:11; Romans 15:13; 16:25-27; 2 Corinthians 1:2-4; 13:14; Jude 24,25. When you have listed and been blessed by the benedictions of the New Testament, then read Numbers 6:22-27 for the benediction God wrote for His people under the law. They opened and closed each day hearing these words recited. Why not recite them aloud before you get up in the morning, and before you lie down at night for one month? At the end of that period, ask yourself: "Am I nearer to my Father now?", "Am I more like Him now?" What are the facts on which I base my answers?

2. Using the sheet of Scriptures in your notebook on Jesus' prayer life, list the Scriptures, then whether or not His position in prayer is recorded and whether He prayed aloud or silently.

3. *God heard* the following persons pray *in unusual places:* List the places.

Hagar (Genesis 16)	Peter (Matthew 14:24-30)
Jonah (Jonah 1-4)	Eleizar (Genesis 24:10-15)
Hezekiah (2 Kings 20:1-3)	Elisha (2 Kings 6:11-17)
David (1 Samuel 22:1,2;	Jesus (Luke 23:46)
Psalm 57;142)	Job (1:20-22)
(2 Samuel 15:30,31)	Paul and Silas (Acts 16)

   Does this study make your faith even stronger in the knowledge that our Father hears us anywhere we are? He is as close as our next breath, as near as a whispered silent prayer.

   > "Whoso draws nigh to God one step
   >   through doubtings dim,
   > God will advance a mile
   >   in blazing light to him."

4. Make a chart:

	Person	Scrip.	Problem	Scrip. Answer
example	Hannah	1 Sam. 1	Childless	
	Paul	2 Cor. 12:7,8	Thorn in flesh	

89

Elijah	1 Kings 17:1
Elijah	1 Kings 18:41-43
Gideon	Judges 6:36
Elisha	2 Kings 4:3
Peter	Acts 9:46
Moses	Numbers 11:15
Samson	Judges 16:30

5. Compare Elijah's brief, pointed, almost abrupt prayers (1 Kings 17:1-11, 2 Kings 2:11) and Daniel's prayers (Daniel 2-12). Can you write out some thoughts on the differences and similarities of their prayers and as a result of your study, then write out the characters of these men their prayers reveal?

6. Study Solomon's prayers. Search out and mark the recorded answers. Did he live to see all of his request fulfilled? Does your study speak to a new insight into your own relationship with God? In what way?

7. Do you pray only at wit's end? What does God have to say about this? Read Psalms 107:27,28. Now read the whole Psalm. What are the conditions of those who cry out? (verses 4,5, 10-12, 17-19, 25-27.)

8. David testifies to the fact of answered prayer: Psalm 40:1-10. If you wrote your testimony, what could you say?

9. Read Moses' prayers: Exodus-Deuteronomy. Notice what a strong leader has to say in intercessory prayers. Were his prayers answered? God makes a touching, revealing statement to Moses—an insight into His own heart about the power of intercessory prayer. (Exodus 32:9,10; Numbers 12:7,8). Don't you love your Father even more for knowing this?

10. Answers that exceed the petitions: 1 Kings 3:7-14; 2 Chronicles 1:10-12; Acts 12:5-15
(Add more of your own research.)

11. Answers to prayer that are different from the request: Deuteronomy 3:23-27; John 11:3,6,43,44; 2 Corinthians 12:8,9

12. Return to your notebooks, and list once more the times Jesus prayed:
1. Where He prayed   2. The Situation   3. Subject of His prayer

13. Are there any prayers in the Bible without answers? I have found none, (except prophetic New Testament prayers). If you locate one please share it with me?

14. A child's prayers are found in 1 Samuel 3. He is _____. Are any other prayers of children recorded?

15. List the prayers of the church found in the book of Acts. How do these prayers speak of the faith of the early church? How could we see this faith among our brothers where we worship?

16. Can you locate a prayer in the Bible that requests something the person praying can accomplish without God's power? Does God/Jesus ever do for people what they can and should do for themselves?

17. *Prayers recorded in the Bible over a wide range of subjects:*
Restoration from the dead: Elijah *1 Kings 7:21;* Elisha *2 Kings 4:3;* Peter *Acts 9:46*
Gideon prayed about a fleece *Judges 6:36*
Isaiah about a sundial *2 Kings 20:11*
Elisha prayed prophetically about a curse *2 Kings 2:24;* for life into a dead son *2 Kings 4:35;* for the foes of Israel to be blind *1 Kings 6:18;* then for the recovery of their sight *2 Kings 6:26*
Hezekiah prayed for the return of health *2 Kings 20:5;* the deliverance from enemy army *2 Kings 19:20*
Elijah prayed for his own death *1 Kings 19:4*
  as did Moses *Numbers 11:15*
  and *Jonah 4:1-9;* Samson *Judges 16:30*
These people prayed about children:
  Isaac pled for Rebekah's conception *Genesis 25:18*
  Rebekah prayed because of a difficult pregnancy *Genesis 28:22*
  Jacob/Israel pronounced a blessing on his grandsons and sons *Genesis 48:20-22; 49:1-28*
  Jephthah prayed a foolish vow *Judges 11:30,31*
  Manoah prayed for parental guidance *Judges 13:8,12*
  Hannah begged for a child to be given to God *1 Samuel 1:10-13,15,17*
  Hannah prayed when she presented Samuel to Eli *1 Samuel 2:1-10*
  David prayed for the little Prince to live *2 Samuel 12:16-19*
  David prayed after the infant's death *2 Samuel 12:20-23*
  Solomon prayed for an understanding heart to judge his people

(God's children) *1 Kings 3:6-9*
Jacob for himself and his family *Genesis 35:2,3,7*
Job for his children *Job 1:5*

Samson prayed for revenge for his blindness (and hopefully meaning the prayer for God's honor also) *Judges 16:28*

David prayed for the counsel of his enemy be turned to foolishness *2 Samuel 15:31*

Abraham's servant prayed to be led to his Master's Son's bride-to-be *Genesis 24:12-14*

Naomi prayed for her dead son's wives to have husbands and children *Ruth 1:8,9* (Oh to have a gracious character, generous like Naomi!)

Conclusion: Compare all these subjects for prayers and Jesus' words Matthew 7:7-11. Is there *anything* you cannot bring to your Father?

18. People of the Bible record prayed for:
    selection of leaders
    about building a worship place
    decisions of all varities
    intercessions for others
    deliverance from oppression
    victory in battle
    to die (Which four men of God?)
    to live
    for removal of maladies (withered limbs, fever, leprosy, blindess, paralysis, sin)

Can you fill in Scripture references for each of these?
Faith! Mark 11:24 "All things" _____

> "Nothing before, nothing behind;
>   The steps of faith
> Fall on the seeming void, and find
>   The rock (Christians would write Rock) beneath."
>   John Greenleaf Whittier

19. Think about the times in your life that you prayed and God blessed you. Write a thanksgiving Psalm to your Father about His boundless love and graciousness. Haven't you found Him to be as He said of Himself (Exodus 34:6,7)? Read what at least four reliable commentaries have to say about these words.

20. Please write me and share some of your learning experiences with

prayer? Let the blessings go out to bring added praise and thanksgiving to the One we adore.

> "He, who from zone to zone,
> Guides through the boundless sky thy certain flight
> In the long way that I must tread alone,
> Will lead my steps aright."
>
> From "To A Waterfowl" by
> William Cullen Bryant
> Thank you, Father-from Me.

Those who left us their prayers in the Scriptures because God selected their words to be there for us, prayed believing that the laws of nature are *not* beyond change, that there is Somebody somewhere Who is strong enough, and caring enough to modify and control the end and its people.

How blessed beyond measure to know that God's hands are strong, loving, sure and perfect! We can entrust ourselves to them, briefly meet, or those who oppose us. Praise His Name!

AMEN